# Table of Contents

S0-BEH-026

**Section Three**
**The Future of the Electoral College**

**Section Four**
**Teaching the Electoral College**

# Picking the President

## Understanding the Electoral College

# PICKING THE PRESIDENT

*Understanding the Electoral College*

*Edited by*
*Eric Burin*

The Digital Press at the University of North Dakota
Grand Forks, ND

Creative Commons License
This work is licensed under a
Creative Commons
By Attribution
4.0 International License.

2017 The Digital Press @ The University of North Dakota
in collaboration with *North Dakota Quarterly*

Book Design: William Caraher
Cover Design: William Caraher

Library of Congress Control Number: 2017901465
Digital Press at The University of North Dakota, The, Grand Forks,
NORTH DAKOTA

ISBN-13: 978-062833445
ISBN-10: 0692833447

# Documents

# Preface

The 2016 presidential election has sparked an unprecedented interest in the Electoral College. In response to Donald Trump winning the presidency despite losing the popular vote, numerous commentators have weighed in with letters-to-the-editor, op-eds, blog posts, and the like, and thanks to the revolution in digital communications, these items have reached an exceptionally wide audience. In short, never before have so many people had so much to say about the Electoral College.

This remains a high-stakes debate, and historians, political scientists, philosophers, and other scholars have an important role to play in it. They can enrich discussions about the Electoral College by situating the system within the history of America and other societies; untangling the intricacies of republicanism, federalism, and democracy; articulating different concepts of political morality; and discerning, through statistical analysis, whom the Electoral College benefits most. In spotlighting the Electoral College from various vantage points, this volume aims to empower citizens to make clear-eyed decisions about it.

If one of this volume's goals is to illuminate the Electoral College, another is to do so while many people are still focused on the topic. This project came together quickly. The entire enterprise went from conception to completion in a mere five weeks. That swiftness was made possible by working with The Digital Press at the University of North Dakota, which embraces a cooperative, transparent model of publication with the goal of producing open-access, electronic works that can attract local and global audiences. Likewise, this volume came to fruition speedily because the contributors agreed to pen brief essays in short order. As a result, while their works have the hallmarks of scholarly articles, they do not constitute an exhaustive examination of the Electoral College. Indeed, many germane subjects are not addressed. Even so, these learned ruminations can enhance the ongoing debate about the Electoral College.

Essays of this sort are much-needed, for the post-election dialogue about the Electoral College has been warped by partisanship. Republicans who reckon that Electoral College benefits their party usually have defended the system. Conversely, Democrats, smarting from the fact that in a span of sixteen years they have twice lost the presidency despite popular vote triumphs, typically have denounced it. This mode of assessment is unfortunate, for it impairs our ability to analyze the Electoral College on its own merits, as opposed to how it affects one party or another. Put another way, the Electoral College is an inherently political institution, but appraisals of it need not be invariably partisan.

To facilitate and expand the conversation about the Electoral College, this volume offers short essays that examine it from different disciplinary perspectives, including philosophy, mathematics, political science, communications, history, and pedagogy. Along the way, the essays address a variety of questions about the Electoral College: Why was it created? What were its antecedents? How has it changed over time? Who benefits from it? Is it just? Should we alter or abolish the Electoral College, and if so, what should replace it? In exploring these matters, *Picking the President* provides timely insights on one of America's most high-profile, momentous issues.

# Introduction

## A Brief History of the Electoral College

Eric Burin

In 1787, Americans probably had more experience writing constitutions than any people ever. They had adopted the Articles of Confederation during the Revolutionary War, and had penned thirteen state constitutions, as well. Perhaps for this reason, it's doubtful anyone arrived at the Constitutional Convention thinking that the Electoral College was the way to pick a president.

Instead, the convention's delegates identified three groups that could select the president: Congress, state governments, or the people. Some delegates (including, at one point, James Madison) favored a popular vote, but many representing slave states or states with restrictive franchise laws objected. Consequently, a good number of attendees championed the congressional option (understandably so, since in most states the legislature elected the governor). This plan nearly triumphed, but a last-minute attempt by South Carolina delegate John Rutledge to privilege the more populous states by having the president be picked by a joint ballot of the Senate *and* House, when combined with a lingering desire to make the executive branch more independent of its legislative counterpart, derailed the proposal. Ultimately, the convention adopted the Electoral College and embedded it in Article II of the Constitution.

Article II is among the most detailed parts of the Constitution and it can be found in its entirety in this volume's Documents section, but it's worthwhile to highlight a few key features here: Under this system, electoral votes were allotted to each state based on the number of Representatives it had in the House, plus its two Senators; state legislatures determined how the electors were picked; each elector could cast two votes for president; and if a presidential candidate failed to get a majority of electoral votes, the House of Representatives, with each state getting one vote, would select the president and vice president from among the top five electoral vote-getters. Several essays in this volume examine why many founders thought this process for picking the president was (to paraphrase Alexander Hamilton) if not a perfect system then at least an excellent one.

After the Constitution was ratified, the Electoral College underwent modifications. These changes were spurred by something the delegates at the Constitutional Convention hadn't anticipated—the rise in the early 1790s of two competing political parties, the Federalists and the Democratic-Republicans. The convention delegates originally envisioned the Electoral College being comprised of knowledgeable and honorable men who, more often than not, would forward to the House a list of commendable, broad-minded presidential candidates, each of whom enjoyed some regional but not national renown. But the infusion of party politics caused the Electoral College to misfire: In 1796, a Democratic-Republican, Thomas Jefferson, ended up serving as vice president to a Federalist president, John Adams. In 1800, Jefferson and his running mate Aaron Burr received the same number of electoral votes, causing a constitutional crisis that nearly led to bloodshed. In response, in 1804, the 12$^{th}$ Amendment was adopted, the most important feature of which was requiring electors to cast separate ballots for the president and vice president. Thereafter, presidential contests became more democratic affairs, essentially morphing into popular referendums on party platforms and the candidates who championed them.

The advent of partisanship also affected the way states selected presidential electors. Early on, most states invested state legislators with that power. But party leaders soon perceived the advantages of adopting statewide, winner-take-all systems (as a case in point, Jefferson's 1796 defeat could be attributed to three solitary Federalist electors who hailed from states that were otherwise in the Democratic-Republican camp). By 1820, the number of states using the statewide system equaled those still using the legislative system. Meanwhile, only a handful of states picked electors by districts. This was the method, Madison wrote in 1823, that the convention delegates had had in mind when they adopted the Electoral College, and consequently he called for an amendment that would have required states to use the district system. Madison's proposal fell on deaf ears, and by 1836, every state except South Carolina had adopted the statewide system. Even so, the sentiment in favor of the district method never expired. In 1966, for example, Delaware, along with eleven other states (including North Dakota), filed suit against New York, arguing that the latter's winner-take-all system effectively disfranchised the less populous states. The U.S. Supreme Court refused to hear the case, and like that ill-fated suit, recent proposals to institute the district method, or hybrid systems like those used in Maine and Nebraska, have made little headway against entrenched political interests.

The collapse of slavery during the Civil War brought to the fore another long-standing political dispute that affected the Electoral College: Which residents should be counted when allocating House seats? Previously, slaveholding states could count three-fifths of their enslaved residents toward their representation in the House. With slavery's demise, newly emancipated African Americans, who at this juncture were not permitted to vote, could now be counted as five-fifths of a person, meaning white southerners' political power was poised to increase during the postbellum period. The emergence in 1867 of Radical Reconstruction, with its commitment to establishing an interracial democracy in the postwar South, resolved this issue, at least temporarily. The enactment of the 14th Amendment in 1868 (which diminished a state's share of House seats proportionally to the extent to which it barred adult male citizens from voting) and the 15th Amendment in 1870 (which prohibited disfranchisement on account of race, color, or previous condition of servitude) effectively granted southern states full representation in the House and the Electoral College on the condition that black men be allowed to vote. By 1900, however, white "redeemers" had seized control of southern governments and disfranchised nearly all black residents with literacy tests, grandfather clauses, and other ostensibly race-neutral mechanisms. As a result, southern states could count African Americans when laying claim to House seats and electoral votes, even though such persons enjoyed virtually no political rights. Many of the redeemers' methods were subsequently outlawed, but disputants still debate how non-voters (such as legal and illegal immigrants, minors, prisoners, and ex-felons) should be counted when distributing House seats and—concomitantly—electoral votes.

The size of the House of Representatives also affects the Electoral College. The Constitution provides little guidance on the matter, only stipulating that 1) apportionment be based on state populations, 2) every state gets at least one Congressperson; and 3) each Congressperson represents no less than 30,000 residents. After the 1790 census, Congress passed a bill that called for 120 House seats, but President George Washington issued a veto—the first veto in U.S. history—with the result being that a subsequent law established the number of seats at 105. Thereafter, Congress almost always increased the number of House seats to keep pace with population growth and the addition of new states into the Union (though there were debates as to how exactly those seats should be divvied up). In 1911, in customary fashion, Congress enacted another apportionment law, this time creating a 433-member House (with a provision that one seat each would be added for Arizona and New Mexico when they became states). Over the next ten years, immigration, migration, and urbanization so altered the nation's demographic landscape that Congresspersons who feared that the next reapportionment would diminish their states' political clout managed to prevent such a law from being passed after the 1920 census. When Congress finally enacted a reapportionment law in 1929, the new statute permanently fixed the number of House seats at 435. Then and now, this cap hurts the most populous states in the House, and by extension, in the Electoral College.

The post-World War II struggle for greater inclusiveness in America brought renewed attention to the Electoral College. The most instrumental change concerned the 23$^{rd}$ Amendment, a measure that allotted electoral votes to the District of Columbia, which was home to 763,000 people. The bill passed Congress in 1960 with considerable bipartisan support, perhaps a reflection of the era's democratic sensibilities, as well as the fact that it wasn't clear whether Republicans or Democrats would win those additional electoral votes. Thereafter, the measure quickly secured the approval of three-quarters of the states. The District's participation in the Electoral College serves as a reminder that many other U.S. possessions are not treated similarly: In the 2016 election, four million Americans (about as many people living in Wyoming, Vermont, Alaska, and North Dakota combined), almost all of them citizens, resided in parts of the U.S., such as Puerto Rico, Guam, and the U.S. Virgin Islands, that were excluded from the Electoral College.

That exclusivity, when combined with the Electoral College's inherently undemocratic nature, has produced results that, in the estimation of some of the system's modern critics, are nearly random, especially when presidential contests feature evenly matched major party candidates and/or strong third-party candidates. For example, in the 1968 race, a good showing by American Independent Party candidate George Wallace and slim margins of victory in key states by Richard Nixon, left many—including Nixon himself—dissatisfied with the Electoral College. In response, Congress took up the Bayh-Celler Amendment, the most serious challenge to the Electoral College to date. This popular vote proposal passed the House but died in the Senate at the hands some small states and many southern ones, where disfranchised African Americans could still be counted when allocating electoral votes. Thereafter, Jimmy Carter's rather contingent and fortuitous victory in 1976 and Ross Perot's notable runs as the Reform Party candidate in 1992 and 1996 inspired additional calls for reform, as did George W. Bush's victory in 2000, in which he won the electoral vote despite losing the popular vote. Similarly, in 2016, Hillary Clinton secured over 2.8 million more votes than Donald Trump, but the latter triumphed in the Electoral College, thanks to narrow victories in a handful of swing states. Such quirks have always been a part of the Electoral College. But in light of the 24th Amendment (which banned the poll tax), the 1965 Voting Rights Act (which established federal protections to safeguard access to the ballot box), the Supreme Court's affirmation of the "one person, one vote" principle, and other advances in political egalitarianism, these an-ti-majoritarian and seemingly unpredictable outcomes are, from the perspective of those who decry the system, disturbingly out of sync with modern sensibilities. As proof, they note that in no other contest do Americans employ anything like the Electoral College. Even so, those who would alter or abolish the Electoral College have a difficult road ahead. Although the system always has been subject to dispute, and opinion polls dating back to the 1940s have shown most Americans preferring a popular vote for president, revising or discarding the Electoral College has proved exceedingly difficult. Moreover, in the immediate aftermath of the 2016 election, the Electoral College became a decidedly partisan issue: Republican support for a constitutional amendment in favor of a popular vote plummeted to 19%, down from 54% in 2011. Furthermore, the 2016 election resulted in Republicans controlling not just the presidency, but also both houses of Congress, 33 governorships, and 68 of 99 state legislative chambers. Given these attitudinal and political conditions, it seems almost certain that the Electoral College will remain embedded in the Constitution for the foreseeable future.

Still, reformers have some cause for optimism. For starters, they can point to the incremental progress of the National Popular Vote Interstate Compact (NPVIC), an arrangement wherein participating states pledge to cast their electoral votes to the winner of the national poplar vote, regardless of the outcome in their particular state. This proposal, which has the advantage of embracing rather than resisting each state's right to determine the means by which it selects presidential electors, would go into effect once the participating states account for a majority of the 538 electoral votes available. As of 2016, ten states, plus the District of Columbia, had signed on. Collectively, they account for 165 electoral votes—61.1% of the 270 needed for the compact to become operational. Those joining the NPVIC thus far have tended to lean strongly Democratic, and there are good reasons to believe that the compact's supporters will encounter more resistance in swing states (which may be unwilling to forego the outsized influence they wield in the Electoral College) and Republican-controlled states (which *currently* oppose alterations to the system). Nevertheless, history shows that attempts at dealing with the Electoral College's alleged defects have made the most headway when it produces especially controversial results, and during periods of partisan tumult and realignment. Such appears to be the case today. These circumstances, when combined with the American ethos of advancement, provide reformers with a glimmer of hope, for as Madison remarked about the means by which Americans pick their president, "a solid improvement of it is a desideratum that ought to be welcomed by all enlightened patriots."

This volume reflects the notion that professional humanists and social scientists have something substantive to offer "enlightened patriots." It is not intended to be a comprehensive survey of the Electoral College, nor does it seek to dictate the terms of debate about the system. Rather, it aims to add perspectives, arguments, and historical evidence. In short, it provides timely, learned responses to one of the most consequential issues of the day, and as such, it endeavors to foster thoughtful, civil discourse among an engaged and informed public.

The essays in Section One put the Electoral College in comparative perspective. **William Caraher** examines how the political institutions of ancient Athens and Rome foreshadowed the Electoral College. **Donald F. Johnson** explores the ways in which the Electoral College mimicked the noble-dominated federal monarchies of early modern Europe. **Manisha Sinha** compares the Electoral College to the "rotten borough" system that existed in Britain until the mid-19th century. **Andrew Meyer** likens the Electoral College to the mechanisms that China adopted to bind together that vast and diverse society. These contributions allow us to see the Electoral College in a new light by placing it side-by-side with comparable political institutions.

The essays in Section Two investigate how the Electoral College has shaped American politics historically. **Andrew Shankman** discusses the ideological assumptions that undergirded the creation of the Electoral College, and the political realities that prompted the ratification of the 12th Amendment. **Patrick Rael** surveys how the Electoral College affected southern political power before and after the Civil War. **Cynthia Culver Prescott** situates the Electoral College's persistence within the larger story of America's halting progress toward equality. **Timothy Prescott** uses statistical analysis to assess the historical relationship between the popular vote and the electoral vote. These works permit us to view contemporary disputes over the Electoral College against the backdrop of the system's long history.

Section Three features five essays that debate the merits of the Electoral College from different disciplinary viewpoints. Philosopher **Jack Russell Weinstein** contemplates whether it is just to have the electoral vote diverge from the popular vote. Communications professor **Mark Trahant** points to the rise of the digital economy and egalitarian values when calling for reforms to the Electoral College and other undemocratic political institutions. Political scientist **Mark Stephen Jendrysik** argues that the Electoral College is an outdated system, and when it produces anti-majoritarian outcomes, it invites a crisis of political legitimacy. Another political scientist, **Benjamin J. Kassow,** warns that any alteration to the Electoral College will necessarily entail important political tradeoffs. Historian **Allen Guelzo** and lawyer **James Hulme** emphasize federalism's virtues in defending the Electoral College. Like the proverbial blind men describing different parts of an elephant, each of these essays provide a distinct perspective on the Electoral College.

In Section Four, **Brad Austin** reflects on how teaching about the historical development of the Electoral College provides an opportunity to cultivate empathy in the classroom. In some ways, his contribution points toward the Documents section at the end of the book. The documents, which are well-known and in the public domain, invite readers to think for themselves about origins and evolution of the Electoral College in the early American republic.

# Section One
# The Electoral College
# in Comparative Perspective

# 1

# Ancient States and Representative Government: Greek and Roman Models for the Electoral College

William Caraher

The framers of the U.S. Constitution looked to antiquity as an inspiration for their own republic. The city-state of Athens during its Classical efflorescence represented a model for democracy, but it was not nearly as compelling as the Roman Republic alternately celebrated by Enlightenment authors and English reformers. Both ancient civilizations offered historical precedents for representative forms of government that allowed the architects of the various colonial and state constitutions, the Articles of Confederation, and the U.S. Constitution to appeals to traditions of government outside and older than the rule of the European aristocracy. Neither the Athenian democracy in its various forms nor the Roman Republic offered an exact precedent for the Electoral College, but both recognized the importance of recognizing regional interests in the context of their popular institutions.

Democratic Athens of the 5th century BC, featured a popular assembly made up of all citizens which generally meant male, property owners, of military age. This assembly met in Athens to vote on whatever legislation that the state required. Over the course of the 7th and 6th centuries BC various institutions served the roles of the executive, generally an office called the archon, and for a range of different judiciary functions. Most importantly for our purpose here, there existed a council responsible for preparing the legislation upon which the popular assembly would vote. In the late 6th century, the Athenian politician Cleisthenes negotiated a series of reforms in Athens including the creation of a "Council of 500" which would serve this function. This council included 50 representatives from each of ten tribes. Each tribe represented communities from each of three non-contiguous regions in Attica, the territory ruled by the city of Athens: the city, the coast, and the interior. The goal of this arrangement was to ensure that each region had representation in the Council of 500 and played a role in the preparation of legislation for the popular assembly (whether this is how this arrangement functioned in practice remains difficult to know). The organization of the Council of 500 around territorially diverse tribes provided an important, representative, counterweight to the popular assembly which tended to be biased toward citizens resident in Athens or who could afford time away from their field, businesses, or jobs to attend voting sessions. In this effort to balance regional concerns with the direct democracy of the assembly, Athens provides an early example of a representative council in the Western tradition. While the tribal basis for the Council of 500 did not ensure each region distinct representation within the Athenian government, it appears to have acknowledged the diverse regional interests present in the Athenian state and it recognized, at least in theory, that compensating for regional interests served as a kind of counterweight to the popular assembly.

Whatever the innovation present in democratic Athens, the Roman Republic provided a far more compelling and influential model for the framers of the U.S. Constitution. Rome, like Athens, did not have a written constitution to guide its governmental structure, but we know enough about how it functioned from historians in antiquity. The Roman Republic possessed an array of assemblies and councils each with specific functions and advantages to particular groups. Unlike Athens, there was far less emphasis on the democratic, popular assembly and a fundamental commitment to the republican practice of voting blocks which represented groups of citizens within Roman society. The two most significant of these councils were the *comitia centuriata* and the *comitia tributa*. In the comitia centuriata, Roman citizens were grouped into first 193 and then 373 centuries according to wealth. Each century was a voting block and the majority of voters within the century decided the vote of that century. The wealthiest citizens were divided into more centuries than the poorest giving them more voting blocks. Moreover, the wealthiest centuries voted first resulting in most elections being decided long before the poorest blocks voted, although reformers consistently tried to shift the balance toward the poorest voters.

The poorest voters tended to congregate in the city of Rome, and this marginalized their political influence in other major assembly, the comitia tributa, which was organized according to region of residence. The city of Rome consisted of four urban tribes whereas the surrounding regions, eventually expanded to include all of Italy, comprised an additional 31. Each of the 35 tribes had a single vote with the 31 rural tribes tending to represent the interests of wealthier, rural landowners. Like in the comitia centuriata, the majority of tribes carried decisions in this assembly. In fact, the politically marginal character of the urban tribes was such that a punishment for certain kind of crimes included moving the guilty individual's tribal affiliation from a rural to an urban tribe to affect a kind of political disenfranchisement. Like in Athens, regional concerns play a role in managing the political balance of the Roman Republic.

While neither the representative council in Cleisthenic Athens or the comitia tributa in republican Rome represented a precise analog to the Electoral College, the Electoral College and the Roman assemblies shared the concept of voting blocks that is, in some appraisals, central to the idea of republican governance. For Rome, the comitia tributa also allowed for the state to expand voting and citizen rights into newly conquered territories while maintaining the privileges of the traditional aristocracy through their control of the majority of tribes. While this may appear to be a regressive tactic designed to conserve the political power of the traditional Roman elite, it also allowed the Roman state to expand political rights to new populations in ways that would have been more politically risky for a direct democracy like in Athens. By slotting new citizens into existing tribes or sequestering them into a small number of tribes, the Roman elite also ensured the stability of the state even during times of expansion.

Today, political commentators like to look to Rome and Athens to predict or make sense of the American political trajectory. This makes sense, of course, because the challenges faced by the Roman Republic and the democracy of Athens allow for sensationally tragic presentations of our country's political fate set amid the fundamental conservatism of the republican political tradition. Whether the U.S. will fail because of this adherence to these outmoded republican practices or find within them stability during times of dynamic change is beyond the limited gaze of the historian's craft.

# 2

## The Electoral College as American Aristocracy

Donald F. Johnson

Although dedicated to creating a republic, for the framers of the United States Constitution a stable aristocracy was essential to the project of crafting a Federal state. Basing their ideas on enlightenment theory and the British constitutional tradition, Constitutional architects such as James Madison and Alexander Hamilton envisioned a strong, independent class of well-educated, wealthy, independent men, who could mimic the function of European nobility and act as a check on potentially tyrannical executives or overly populist legislative assemblies. The Senate, meant to be a republican version of the British House of Lords, was perhaps the most obvious attempt at enshrining the interests of these wealthy men in government at the national level. The Electoral College, however, was crucial in creating a functioning local aristocracy in America. And, unlike the Senate, it is one that has never been democratized, maintaining to this day its connections to the monarchial governments of early modern Europe upon which it was based.[1]

Indeed, if the Senate was meant to establish a national aristocracy, the framers intended for the Electoral College to maintain elite representation at the state and local levels. The Constitution prescribed no form of selection for state electors, and did not bind

---

[1] On the importance of mixed government for the framers, see James Madison, *Federalist* No. 40 and Alexander Hamilton, *Federalist* Nos. 23-28. For their Enlightenment inspiration, see Locke, *Two Treatises on Government* (1689) and Montesquieu, *On the Spirit of the Laws* (1748). On the Senate as safely fulfilling the aristocratic function in a mixed republican government, see Madison, Alexander Hamilton, and John Jay, *Federalist* Nos. 62-66.

them to follow popular elections for president in any way. As the Alexander Hamilton's *Federalist* No. 68 demonstrates, the College was meant to be a check on the excesses of the people, comprised of wealthy men "free from any sinister bias" who would protect the presidency from falling into the hands of "any man who is not in an eminent degree endowed with the requisite qualifications." Hamilton, Madison, and other Federalists assumed that state-level elites would act as a further check on the powers of the people and of demagogues who might seduce them. Still, such a blatantly un-representative feature seems out-of-place in a representative form of government.[2]

This dissonance is because the Electoral College was based not on republican theory but on the structure of aristocratic elective monarchies in eighteenth-century Europe, most notably the Dutch Republic, the Commonwealth of Poland-Lithuania, and the Holy Roman Empire. In the Netherlands, representatives from seven feudal provinces, each administered independently by hereditary lords, gathered periodically to elect a stadholder, or steward, responsible for leading the Dutch army in wartime, administering foreign affairs, and resolving conflicts between the provinces. Typically, stadholders came from the House of Orange, which became the de-facto royal family of the Netherlands (and whose most prominent member, William III, ascended the throne of Great Britain in 1688). Nevertheless, through the electoral system nobles of each province maintained autonomy over their provinces.

In early modern Poland-Lithuania, nobles came together from tens of thousands of sovereign fiefs to elect new monarchs upon the death of a prior king. Meeting in the sjem, or noble Parliament, these aristocrats tended to elect members of prominent families from among their own ranks, though elections could be bitterly disputed and more than once led to schisms and civil wars. Still, as in the Dutch Republic, the sjem ensured that nobles maintained power within their domains, and exercised supervisory authority over their executive.

---

[2] For the selection of electors, see the United States Constitution, Article II, Section 1. For Hamilton's analysis, see Hamilton, *Federalist* No. 68 in the Documents section.

Finally, the Holy Roman Empire comprised perhaps the oldest and most well-known electoral college. For almost a thousand years, seven to ten electors of various German and Italian states comprising the Empire met periodically to elect a new Emperor, who usually came from the Hapsburg dynasty of Austria. Despite its seeming stability, however, electoral politics in the Empire were fraught with religious and political intrigue, and prince-electors (of whom George III of Great Britain, in his dual capacity as ruler of Hanover, was one) exercised near total autonomy over their own domains.[3]

The American Electoral College thus resembles more closely those of noble-dominated Federal monarchies of late-eighteenth century Europe than the British-style mixed constitution from which the framers drew much of their inspiration. electors, drawn from the elites of each state in the Union, would confirm not only the integrity of the Presidency but also maintain the power of the local aristocracies in each region of the country. Yet, while the electoral systems of the Netherlands, Poland, and the Holy Roman Empire were destroyed in Revolutionary fervor during the 1790s and 1800s, the American Electoral College persists in much the same form established in 1789.

Indeed, the Electoral College continues to perpetuate a regional American aristocracy. Unlike the Senate, which was reformed in 1913 to allow for direct elections, electors are still appointed by state legislatures and governors, and typically comprise local elites. 2016 electors for the state of New York, for example, included former President Bill Clinton, current governor Andrew Cuomo, and current New York City Mayor Bill de Blasio.[4] Given its noble origins in pre-Revolutionary Europe and recent dramatic splits between the electoral and popular votes, perhaps further consideration of its place in modern American society is in order.

---

[3] For more on the composition of the Holy Roman Empire, Poland, and the Netherlands in the early modern period, see Thomas Ertman, *Birth of the Leviathan: Building States and Regimes in Medieval and Early Modern Europe* (Cambridge, 1997).

[4] "Duly Appointed Presidential Electors." *The Green Papers: 2016 General Election*, accessed December 27th, 2016; http://www.thegreenpapers.com/G16/EC-Electors.phtml.

# 3

## America's Rotten Electoral College System

Manisha Sinha

Something stinks about the recent presidential election. It emanates from the country's rotten Electoral College system for selecting the president of the United States. I use the term rotten advisedly. America's Electoral College in the twenty-first century resembles Britain's "rotten borough" system of electing members of Parliament in the eighteenth and nineteenth centuries. Not only was the franchise restricted to an elite but "rotten boroughs" with very few voters could elect representatives to Parliament like the far more populous industrializing urban centers. With the Great Reform Acts of 1832 and of the 1860s, Britain adopted universal manhood suffrage and did away with rotten boroughs. But the United States persists in retaining its undemocratic and clunky Electoral College.

When the framers of the Constitution devised the office of the presidency as a republican stand-in for the British monarch and indirect presidential elections through an Electoral College, they did so as a check on democracy. Each state was rewarded the same number of electoral votes as their congressional delegation, giving small states that had equal number of senators as larger states and slaveholding states that received greater representation in the House of Representatives because of the three-fifths clause, greater electoral weight in the presidential elections. The anti-democratic nature of selecting the president was amplified by most states, which initially had their legislatures rather than their voters select presidential electors. With the spread of Jacksonian democracy, adult white men got the right to vote for presidential electors except for one hold out, South Carolina until the Civil War.

Constitutional purists who want to retain the Electoral College must recall that American democracy has progressed through constitutional amendments. The blueprint for presidential elections has proven to be one of the Constitution's most inefficient sections. One of the earliest constitutional amendments, the 12th, clarified that electoral votes for the presidency and vice presidency must be distinct. The demise of slavery mandated by the 13th amendment, and with it the three-fifths clause that gave slaveholders such a powerful say in government, made political representation in the United States more equitable. The expansion of suffrage for African Americans and women through constitutional amendments, the 14th, 15th, and 19th amendments and the Voting Rights Act of 1965 were important milestones in the growth of American democracy.

The cumbersome Electoral College however has remained in place, partly because its undemocratic nature has not been so egregiously showcased as in the recent presidential elections. Before 2016, only four times in American history has the winner of the popular presidential vote not won the Electoral College. The most recent instance until this year was the contested Gore-Bush presidential elections of 2000. But this year, the candidate who lost the Electoral College, Hillary Clinton, won the popular vote overwhelmingly, by nearly three million votes, the largest margin ever for the loser of the Electoral College. These results discredit the Electoral College system that weights voters in certain areas more than others and makes many of the states in the heartland and the South the "rotten boroughs" of today. It calls into question the democratic legitimacy of the presidential elections. Over two hundred years ago, American patriots rejected "virtual representation" in the British Parliament for self-government. That tenuous experiment in republican government has survived only by expanding the boundaries of democracy. It is high time then that we got rid of the rotten borough Electoral College system of electing presidents of the United States.

# 4

## The South (or the North, or the West...) Will Rise Again, and Again, and Again: Viewing the Electoral College from the Perspective of Chinese History*

Andrew Meyer

On July 20, 1842, during the Opium War, British soldiers and warships captured the garrison town of Zhenjiang, at the juncture of the Yangzi River and the Grand Canal in the Qing Empire's Jiangsu Province. When news reached the Daoguang Emperor (r. 1821-1850) in Beijing, he authorized his emissaries to treat for peace. Though Qing resistance up to that point had been robust, the capture of Zhenjiang gave the British control of a fatal fracture point in the larger imperial edifice.

With the Grand Canal blocked, little tax revenue could flow from the southern reaches of the empire to the capital. Two-thirds of the population of the Qing empire lived south of the Yangzi, and the economic disparity south-to-north was even greater than the demographic one. The per capita GDP of the agriculturally and commercially rich southern Jiangnan region was nearly twice that of more arid, sparsely populated northern districts like Qinghai and Gansu. The revenue system of the Qing, which drew tax receipts into the capital on the North China Plain, served as a wealth-transfer mechanism from the wealthy south to the impoverished north. Disrupting that flow for any length of time could cause the precarious social contract holding the empire together to unravel.

---

*A version of this essay appeared as Andrew Meyer, "The South (or the North, or the West...) Will Rise Again, and Again, and Again: Viewing the Electoral College from the Perspective of Chinese History," *Madman of Chu* (blog), November 22, 2016, http://madmanofchu.blogspot.com/2016/11/the-south-or-north-or-west-will-rise.html

In the wake of the Opium War the worst fears of the Qing government were realized. In Guangzhou (Canton) in 1837, the young scion of a southern gentry family, Hong Xiuquan (1814-1864) had for the second time sat for and failed the imperial exams that were the surest route to political, economic and social success. The pass rates on the exams were extraordinarily low throughout the empire, but the odds were made even worse for southerners like Hong by the imposition of quotas favoring candidates from disadvantaged northern regions. His rage and frustration at this second failure induced a nervous collapse: he fell into a feverish state in which he had prophetic visions. After the Opium War he came to understand these visions as a divine calling and began to gather followers. The movement that he began eventually threw the Qing Empire into civil war, with large parts of southern China breaking away to form the Taiping Heavenly Kingdom from 1850 to 1864. Unity was only restored after conflict that left as many as 20 million people dead and the economy of the empire shattered.

The Taiping Rebellion is only one (though admittedly among the worst) of the many instances of cataclysmic breakdown experienced within the Chinese empire over the 2+ millennia of its history that were, in part, induced by inter-regional tensions and conflicts. Successive imperial regimes struggled to hold together an expansive domain throughout which social and economic capital was unevenly distributed. Though Chinese leaders developed and maintained redistributive mechanisms to offset regional disparities (for example, the quotas favoring northern candidates in the imperial exams), these were not generally elastic and responsive enough to relieve the persistent centrifugal forces driving the component regions of the empire apart. The problem, moreover, remains an urgent concern today, as attested by the recent unrest over Beijing's refusal to allow two secessionist legislators to be sworn in as members of the Hong Kong Legislative Council.

This history poses lessons for those of us contemplating the issue of the Electoral College in the wake of the 2016 election. Not only has the Electoral College subverted the results of the popular vote for the second time in less than twenty years, but the 2016 race has yielded an unprecedented disparity between popular and electoral vote outcomes. Hillary Clinton won the popular vote by 2.86 million votes (a 2.1% lead) and lost the Electoral College by 74 votes (a 23% deficit). That the relative differential between the two vote tallies should be so wide understandably creates a sense of profound unfairness—the impression that the democratic will of the people has been effaced by an arcane institution.

Though there will be renewed calls for the abolition of the Electoral College, the historical experience of China should give us pause to wonder at the wisdom of such a course. Like China, the United States is a vast and diverse domain in which social and economic capital are unevenly distributed and the interests of different groups vary widely from region to region. The 2016 election has starkly highlighted the regional tensions straining our social fabric, with voters in the industrial Midwest and rural Appalachia mobilizing to deliver an electoral result that radically undermined conventional expectations. Donald Trump would not have won this election unless poor- and working-class voters in states like Michigan, Pennsylvania, Ohio, North Carolina and Wisconsin had defected from the Democratic Party in favor of his disruptive campaign, and that movement would not have resulted in a Trump victory absent the auspices of the Electoral College.

This being the case, as predictably as there is and will remain pressure to dismantle the Electoral College, there will be strong resistance to any campaign in this direction. To understand why, it is useful to contemplate what a presidential campaign would look like if such contests were decided purely by the popular vote. Candidates would focus almost entirely on the densely populated coasts to the exclusion of the interior, and on urban centers to the exclusion of more sparsely settled rural districts. By giving disproportionate leverage to more rural and sparsely populated states, the Electoral College forces candidates to wage truly national campaigns and to float policies that can win the votes of more marginalized citizens.

The 2016 election provides an object lesson in these redistributive dynamics. Hillary Clinton won the popular vote in California by 4.26 million votes. Thus if one eliminates California's total from the national tally, Donald Trump wins the national popular vote by 1.4 million votes. This is a reflection of the fact that the Electoral College weights the popular vote of smaller and less densely populated states heavily, such that a vote cast in West Virginia is worth three times that of a vote cast in California. While that disparity might seem strangely arbitrary, to citizens in West Virginia, which has a per capita GDP of $38,567, it no doubt feels very fair that their votes should count more than those of their compatriots in California, who enjoy a per capita GDP of $61,924. In light of these facts we can see that in the 2016 election, the system as currently constituted has (or at least will be perceived as having) delivered a shocking victory to rural and industrial working-class voters over coastal elites; one that they would never have achieved in the absence of the Electoral College. For this reason, any move to eliminate this institution will be perceived as an attempt at the kind of "rigging" so loudly decried by the more acrimonious rhetoric of the recent campaign.

As votes continue to be counted and Hillary Clinton's lead in the popular vote widens, anger at the mechanics of the Electoral College will no doubt increase. In contemplating the situation, however, we must clearly understand that the elimination of the Electoral College cannot be taken for granted as an obvious "fix" to a quaintly arcane and obsolete institution. Reversion to the popular vote to decide presidential elections is and would be a drastically radical change to our larger social contract, one that materially impacts the interests of millions of citizens and significantly redistributes power across the political terrain. There are good philosophical arguments to be made against the "unfairness" of the Electoral College, but the historical experience of China demonstrates that there are likewise good practical and even ethical arguments on the other side of the issue. We must acknowledge and account for all of the consequences of changing the current system as we debate the issue moving forward, and undertake any such discussion in a spirit of extreme sensitivity to the interests of *all* groups that would be affected by any reform.

# Section Two
# The Electoral College
# in Historical Perspective

# 5

## What the Founders Were Thinking:
## Why We have the Electoral College[*]

Andrew Shankman

Never in our lifetimes has the Electoral College commanded so much attention. In arguing about what the Founders' original intent was in creating it, and whether electors would defect from their state's popular vote, supporters and opponents of Donald Trump have shown little knowledge of the Electoral College's history. Both sides do not understand that the Founders' Electoral College quickly became a source of chaos, causing the nation to abandon it fifteen years after ratifying the Constitution. The second version of the Electoral College that replaced the first in 1804 solved a destructive problem, but created a new and likely fatal one that we have lived with ever since. Now that the electoral vote has diverged from the popular vote in 40% of the elections conducted during the twenty-first century, the problem is nearing a crisis. We need a clearer understanding of the origins and history of the Electoral College to understand why it is contributing to our current bitter division—and what we should do about it.

Created by the Constitution, the original Electoral College worked like this: each state appointed electors equal to its number of senators (2) plus representatives, apportioned at a ratio of 1 for every 30,000 residents. Each elector cast two votes for president and at least one of those votes had to be for someone outside the elector's state. If someone received the most votes and a majori-

---

[*] A version of this essay appeared as Andrew Shankman, "What Were the Founders Thinking When They Created the Electoral College?" *History News Network*, November 28, 2016, http://historynewsnetwork. org/article/164514

ty, he became president. The second highest vote-getter became vice president. If no one received a majority, the decision went to the House of Representatives, which could choose the president from among the top five vote-getters, and had to make the highest vote-getter vice president if they chose not to make him president. To us these original procedures may sound insane; in 2016, they would make majority vote-getter Donald Trump president and Hillary Clinton vice president.

So, what were the Founders thinking? The Founders were inspired by the classical republics of Greece and Rome and believed they had collapsed when they stopped seeking the public good as their citizens divided into parties to pursue their own interests. For the Founders the public good emerged from a coherent set of values, and understanding how to achieve it required a deep knowledge of the classics, of natural law, common law, and the law of nations, and of the new science of political economy that arose during the Enlightenment. Above all, one had to possess disinterested virtue--putting aside personal interests for the sake of the public good. The Founders thought that most citizens were not capable of fully comprehending the public good. For the United States to succeed, the small group of great and talented men who could would have to guide them. Believing in a unifying singular public good, the Founders saw no value in political parties. Parties existed to promote competing interests, which was contrary to the public good. Citizens either embraced the public good or they behaved selfishly and badly.

Only by starting with these assumptions did the Electoral College make sense. After George Washington's presidency, the Founders assumed their Electoral College would routinely place the decision of who would be president with the House of Representatives. They reasoned that the small group capable of comprehending the public good was evenly distributed geographically. A reasonable number of them would stand for election. Each would be equally qualified virtuous gentlemen. Without political parties to inflame passions and mobilize voters into a few large groups, only rarely would a candidate gain majority support in the Electoral College. The Electoral College would helpfully sort out five from the larger group of the equally qualified, but usually would do little more than that.

Yet almost immediately after ratification of the Constitution, reality obliterated the Founders' plan. Bitter divisions over Hamilton's financial system and the French Revolution showed that Americans violently disagreed with each other. By 1796 two political parties had formed to support or oppose the current course of the nation's domestic and foreign policies and to compete for the presidency. Divided Founders became adversarial party leaders. With large regional, even national, voting blocks, it was suddenly highly likely that the leader of one of the two parties would gain a majority in the Electoral College. The Electoral College would now do what the Founders never imagined it should routinely do—determine the presidency. And the new president's most powerful critic, the leader of the opposition party, would likely get the second most electoral votes, become the vice president, and bring bitter partisan rancor into the heart of the executive branch. This bizarre outcome happened in 1796 when Federalist John Adams was elected president due to receiving the majority of electoral votes, and his opponent, Democratic-Republican Thomas Jefferson, became vice president. In 1800 Jefferson's electors were so disciplined that they cast each of their two votes for him and for Aaron Burr, who they planned to make vice president. The result was that both received the same number of votes while finishing ahead of their Federalist opponents, leading to a prolonged constitutional crisis during which Pennsylvania's Governor contemplated marching his state militia to Washington D.C. to prevent anyone other than Jefferson from being inaugurated.

By 1800 democracy and political parties had made the Electoral College an instrument of chaos. It led in 1804 to passage of the Twelfth Amendment, which required that electors stipulate a vote for president and for vice president. In abandoning the Founders' vision for the Electoral College, Americans were admitting that they did not live in the sort of republic where the Founders' Electoral College made sense: one where virtuous gentlemen pursued the singular unifying public good about which they all agreed. In altering the Electoral College as they did, Americans of the early nineteenth century left us a hybrid and confused version of the original. Requiring electors to vote for a president and a vice president on a single ticket was a concession that party political conflict was never going away. Yet though political parties and democratic conflict were now acknowledged to be the driving force in American politics—that getting the most votes was what mattered—those parties would simply have to trust to luck that their votes were distributed in just the right way to gain an electoral majority.

Over time the Electoral College has become increasingly dysfunctional. As the nation's population grew, in the twentieth century we limited the number of representatives to 435 to prevent the House of Representatives from becoming absurdly large. The total number of electoral votes is capped at 538 (senators plus representatives plus three votes for the District of Columbia) and 153 are distributed away immediately since all states must have a minimum of three. The remaining 385 are distributed by population, which grows ever more distorting as the 385 total remains constant while the population grows. In 2014 California's population amounted to 66 Wyomings. Wyoming has three electors and California 55. But to ensure that a vote from California counted as much as one from Wyoming, California would need 199.

The hybridized confusion has led to our current schizophrenia. Trump supporters demanded that electors obey the popular vote within their states. At the state level the popular vote must be respected so that at the national level the popular vote can be ignored. This selective devotion to the popular vote is a legacy of the confusion that resulted when the Founders created an institution that made sense only for conditions that it quickly turned out did not exist. In 1803 Americans merged the Electoral College, an institution that only made sense in a world without partisanship and organized political parties, with a political process and a political culture based on partisan conflict organized by political parties. Rather than allow chronic chaos in their Republic, the Americans of 1803 abandoned the Founders' Electoral College. To avoid chronic chaos in our Republic, we must abandon the Electoral College entirely.

# 6

## Did Disenfranchisement Give the South an Electoral Advantage?*

Patrick Rael

There has been much recent discussion of the three-fifths clause of the Constitution,[1] which boosted slaveholding states' representation in the Electoral College by including for apportionment a population that received no benefits from government. Scholars have debated how this influenced national politics under slavery, but this conversation applies to the post-emancipation world as well.[2]

Let us start in 1860. With the three-fifths clause operating, the slaveholding states controlled 120 of 303 electoral votes (EV), or 40%. The free states desired a "0/5" scenario, in which slaveholding states received no representation benefit for the enslaved population. In this case, the South would have controlled only 35% of all EV. In 1860, the three-fifths clause thus gave the South a substantial 5% bump.[3]

---

* A version of this essay appeared as Patrick Rael, "Did Disenfranchisement Give the South an Electoral Advantage?" *Journal of the Civil War Era* (blog), December 13, 2016, http://journalofthecivilwarera. org/2016/12/disenfranchisement-give-south-electoral-advantage/.
[1] For a brief summary see: Wikipedia contributors, "Three-Fifths Compromise," *Wikipedia, The Free Encyclopedia.* Accessed December 31, 2016. https://en.wikipedia.org/w/index.php?title=Three-Fifths_Compromise&oldid=754867751.
[2] See, for example, "Slavery, Democracy, and the Racialized Roots of the Electoral College," AAIHS (November 14, 2016); "Is slavery the reason for the Electoral College?" CNN.com (November 22, 2016); "Yes, The Electoral College Really Is A Vestige Of Slavery. It's Time To Get Rid Of It." WGBH News (December 6, 2016).
[3] All figures based on my analysis of data from *Historical Statistics of the*

Under the South's desired "5/5" scenario — the one in which all slaves counted for representation — the South would have controlled 42% of all EV. That is a more modest bump of 2% (about 7 EV) over what it actually enjoyed under the 3/5 ratio.

Emancipation enhanced the South's share of national power by propelling 3.9 million former slaves into the ranks of the population used as a basis for apportionment. With slavery gone, each former bondsperson would now be counted as a whole person rather than three-fifths of one. In principle, this was a "5/5" scenario, in which all people (former slaves among them) were considered for purposes of representation.

In the 1872 election cycle, which was the first to rely on post-emancipation census figures, the South controlled 138 of 366 (38%) EV. Had former slaves not been included (a "0/5" scenario), the South would have controlled only 90 of 319 (29%) EV. The emancipated freedpeople thus gave the South a 9% bump in representation in the Electoral College.

It was good that emancipation boosted southern political power so long as those added to the apportionment population had access to the political process through the 14th and 15th Amendments, which granted citizenship to African Americans, and the franchise to black men. But under conditions of complete disfranchisement, which southern states came close to making around the turn of the 20th century, no African Americans received direct representation in Congress.[4] At that point, emancipation's boost in

---

*United States, Earliest Times to the Present: Millennial Edition*, Susan B. Carter, Scott Sigmund Gartner, Michael R. Haines, Alan L. Olmstead, Richard Sutch, and Gavin Wright, eds. (New York: Cambridge University Press, 2006); "Inter-university Consortium for Political and Social Research. Historical, Demographic, Economic, and Social Data: the United States, 1790-1970 (ICPSR 3)," [Computer file] (Ann Arbor, MI: Inter-University Consortium for Political and Social Research, 197?). A note of caution: there are many ways of building counterfactual scenarios with these numbers. I have made some plausible but not airtight assumptions, such as that the apportionment basis for each cycle would not change despite having fewer people in the apportionment population. Bottom line: republish these numbers at your own risk.

[4] Absolute disfranchisement was the goal, but it was rarely complete.

Southern power worked (some might say ironically) against African Americans, who struggled against racist state regimes whose disproportionate strength in national government blacks' presence was artificially inflating. Imagine trying to get federal anti-lynching legislation passed against Southern states that had worked to remove blacks from the voting population, and were stronger than they should've been because of it.

By 1900, African Americans were being largely expelled from the political process. Their concerns went unrepresented, and yet their numbers still boosted Southern representation in the Electoral College. Effectively, the country ran on the "5/5" principle even though the reality was that close to "0/5" of blacks could vote for their own representatives.

In slavery, this desire had resulted in the diminishment of Southern power. At the constitutional convention in 1787, representatives from northern states had bargained the South down to counting only three-fifths of each slave for representation. After the war, Republicans had sought to carry this principle into freedom by Section 2 of the 14th Amendment, which provided for the diminishment of a state's enumerated population in proportion to the proportion of voters it disenfranchised. That failed, though, as did the 15th Amendment's voting protections, when the Supreme Court began (from the 1870s on) permitting ostensibly race-neutral but intentionally race-specific disfranchisement measures. This gave white supremacists the best of both worlds — they received the enhanced political power that went with a larger population, without the obligation to serve that population.

The numbers for 1900 bear this out. In the "5/5" reality, the states that had held slaves in 1860 ("the South") had 159 EV, or 35% of the total. Under a "0/5" scenario, in which the South would lose representation for the blacks it refused to enfranchise, the South would have had only 112 EV, or 28% of a smaller House.

The South thus gained a lot from disenfranchisement. At the turn of the century, its largely disenfranchised African Americans gave it a 7% bump in the Electoral College, which was one even

---

I make no claims here about how many were *actually* disenfranchised. This is about hypothetical extremes.

### North v. South in the Electoral College: Scenarios

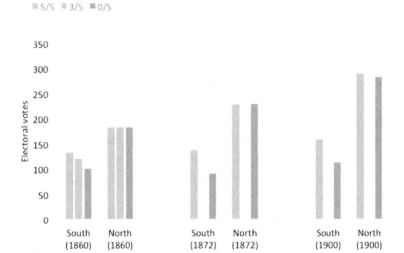

Information from Susan B. Carter et al., eds., *Historical Statistics of the United States, Earliest Times to the Present: Millennial Edition* (New York: Cambridge University Press, 2006).

larger than the 4-5% bump the three-fifths clause usually gave under slavery. And, as before the war, this was a population included *only* to boost representation, for it could make virtually no claim on the political process at all.

The Electoral College has always provided the ruleset for selecting the President of the United States. The framers of the Constitution hoped that this membrane between the voters and the office of President would insulate the electoral process from the "heats and ferments" of public opinion, as Alexander Hamilton put it in *Federalist* No. 68.[5] But the cost has been high, for anti-democratic politicians have always been willing to game the system. One might have thought that ending slavery would have ended the compromise embodied in the three-fifths clause — a system that John Quincy Adams came to call "morally and politically vicious."[6] It was not to be. Of the many paradoxes to the

---

[5] James Madison, *Federalist* No.68, see the Documents section.

[6] Josiah Quincy, *Memoir of the Life of John Quincy Adams* (Boston: Crosby, Nichols, Lee and Co., 1860), 108-9.

"freedom" that followed slavery, one of the most neglected may be this: in the era of Jim Crow, ending slavery only made the white South stronger.

# 7

## Citizenship, Civil Rights, and Electoral Politics

Cynthia Culver Prescott

The United States is a democratic meritocracy. Or so we like to believe. While the general trajectory has been toward greater political and social equality, progress has been uneven. Government policies have made the American dream open to many, while disadvantaging or deliberately excluding others. The American West has long been imagined as land of rugged egalitarianism, but white settlement actually exacerbated inequality in important ways. Although the U.S. has had an egalitarian streak since its founding, Americans have also deep reservations about sharing power equitably. This enduring tension between egalitarianism and deep-seated distrust of the American people may help explain the resilience of the remarkably undemocratic Electoral College.

In the decades following our nation's founding, many people residing within the boundaries of the United States did not qualify as citizens entrusted with the vote. Property laws and poll taxes ensured that only the worthiest – read: wealthiest and whitest – men could vote. white women were counted for representation purposes in the legislature and the Electoral College, but they could not vote. Under coverture, married women's legal personhood was absorbed by her husband. Native Americans and African Americans, among others, enjoyed few rights. And, of course, slaves were only counted as three-fifths of a person for representation purposes, and were treated as chattel rather than as citizens with political rights.

Over the past two hundred years, our nation has expanded the privileges of citizenship to more and more Americans. African Americans gained citizenship in 1868 and Native Americans in 1924. Women gained the right to vote in 1920. African American suffrage was enshrined in the Constitution in 1870; nearly a century later, the Voting Rights Act of 1965 removed legal barriers against Blacks exercising the franchise. We have made our representative democracy more direct over the past two centuries, particularly through the direct election of senators (1913). Initiative, referendum and recall powers were also introduced in many states during the early twentieth century.

Viewed in this context of expanding political rights and greater power for American voters, the Electoral College system appears anachronistic. But our nation's path toward inclusivity has not been as smooth, nor our inclusivity as complete, as we like to believe.

During the nineteenth century, American women steadily gained political and economic rights. But when women were granted suffrage or married women the right to own property separate from their husbands, those gains were often motivated not by a belief in women's equality, but out of male self-interest. Granting women rights became a means to strengthen a particular group's political influence, or to protect familial property. And only native-born white women benefitted from many of these privileges.

Following the Civil War, Radical Republicans sought to reconstruct the social fabric of the South, including granting citizenship and suffrage to African Americans. But those gains were short-lived, as white southerners adopted Jim Crow laws, literacy tests, and other means to limit African-American rights. The 1965 Voting Rights Act finally outlawed these discriminatory practices, but in recent years laws supposedly targeting voter fraud have suppressed voter participation among people of color and both the rural and urban poor.

Third U.S. President (and elite slaveholder) Thomas Jefferson envisioned a nation of yeoman farmers that would serve as the basis of American democracy. A century later, historian Frederick Jackson Turner similarly declared that the western frontier's wide open spaces and supposedly free land formed the basis of American democracy. Many nineteenth-century Americans agreed, and this vision shaped many aspects of federal policy for generations. For example, Jeffersonian agrarianism motivated both the Louisiana Purchase and the Homestead Act. But like our history of expanding civil rights, the legacy of Jefferson's vision is complex. Only people of some means could afford to migrate west to claim land. More than half of claimants failed to prove up on their land. Western lands often wound up in the hands of speculators rather than family farmers. Moreover, white settlement in the West was predicated on the forced removal of native peoples. Indigenous peoples' lives were disrupted or destroyed to enable certain whites to become good democratic citizens.

But even as the U.S. government fought wars and displaced Native Americans to ensure a nation of independent men, many Americans distrusted those western democrats. Painter George Caleb Bingham captured this tension in his famous 1852 painting *The County Election*. Although a blue banner declares "The will of the people is the supreme law," the raucous scene highlights the influence of party politics, money, alcohol use, and even violence on voters – all of them white men, of course. Young boys play with a knife in the dirt and a stray dog wanders through the crowd, but women and people of color are excluded from participation.

Bingham's painting celebrated the participation of white men from different social classes in western elections. But participation by both wealthy businessmen and workingmen does not mean that nineteenth-century elections were egalitarian. Party-specific tickets were cast publicly. *Viva voce* voting persisted in some states. While speaking their choices out loud rather than marking a paper ballot made it possible for illiterate men to participate, it also made them particularly vulnerable to pressure from the political and economic elites.

American agrarian ideals were redefined in the twentieth century. Rather than dreaming of owning an independent family farm, Americans increasingly dreamed of owning a ranch home surrounded by a green lawn in the suburbs. Homeownership replaced homestead ownership at the core of the American dream. Like nineteenth-century land claim laws, government policies enabled wealthier white Americans to buy homes in these suburbs at the expense of others.

For all our faith in Jeffersonian agrarianism as the basis of a free, democratic society, Americans have remained suspicious of the people who make up that republic. Perhaps this tension between trust and distrust explains our pendulum swings between growing civil rights and disfranchisement, and our continued reliance on the Electoral College. Ironically, western lands that were supposed to breed democracy instead have become among the most inequitably treated under the Electoral College system. Due to uneven population distribution, ethnically diverse California and Texas voters are grossly underrepresented in the Electoral College, while heavily white Wyoming and North Dakota voters are overrepresented. And nearly all western states have become among the most reliably "red" or "blue," thus limiting their impact on the presidential election. In recent presidential elections, the Electoral College system has ensured that a few "battleground states" – and especially white suburban men and women – have determined the outcome of the presidential election. In 2016, rural Americans in Midwestern "swing states" consistently voted for Donald Trump, while urban populations supported Hillary Clinton. white suburbanites proved to be the swingiest of swing voters, and they won the Electoral College for Trump, despite Clinton's two percent advantage in the popular vote. Our policies ensured that white suburban homeowners living in an earlier trans-Appalachian West would select the next President of the United States.

Americans are not as equal nor as egalitarian as we like to believe. The persistent tension between egalitarianism and distrust of individuals (especially women and ethnic minorities) contributed to our uneven progress toward social equality, and may help to explain the tenacity of the unequal Electoral College system.

# 8

## Quantifying a Candidate's Advantage in the Electoral College

Timothy Prescott

The Electoral College currently functions as a compromise between big states (who would like to see votes weighted proportionally to their population, as in the House of Representatives) and small states (who would like each state to count equally, as in the Senate). Nationally, there are about 600,000 people for each elector. But in the most extreme example of this weighting, Wyoming, there are just under 200,000, so that each Wyoming resident is about three times as powerful on the national stage.

Despite this, the biggest reason for the disparity between the popular vote and the Electoral College is the fact that every state, except for Nebraska and Maine, awards all of its electors to the winner of that state. This means that a candidate could hypothetically lose the popular vote 25% to 75%, but because they eked out victories in over half of the states, they could still win the Electoral College. In fact, by concentrating on less populous states (currently the 40 smallest), it is possible to push this down to winning with less than 23% of the popular vote.

This leads us to consider how candidates have historically done in the Electoral College as compared to the national popular vote (assuming all electors vote as pledged). As the national popular vote increases, we'll distribute the votes proportional to that candidate's eventual support in each state, with each state and its electors tipping one by one to the candidate's side when the distributed votes eclipses the opponent's eventual total. The state that finally provides the candidate with a majority in the Electoral College determines the election. We'll call that state the *clinching state*, and the difference between the clinching state's margin of victory and the candidate's actual margin of victory their *electoral advantage*.

For example, in the 2016 election, Donald Trump won the Electoral College by 74 votes, but lost the popular vote by 2.09%. He could have lost Michigan and Pennsylvania and still won the Electoral College by 2 votes; it was Wisconsin with its margin of .76% that clinched the Electoral College. Therefore, Trump could have done .76% worse, lost the popular vote by 2.85%, and it would have been Wisconsin that clinched the election. We will say that this means Donald Trump had a 2.85% electoral advantage.

In contrast, in 2004 Bush won the popular vote by 2.46%. If he had done 2.11% worse in every state, he would have won the popular vote by .35%, lost Iowa and New Mexico, and the winner of Ohio would have clinched the Electoral College. We'll say that this means Bush had a .35% electoral disadvantage (or a -.35% electoral advantage). (In our hypothetical examples, the winning candidate had a 50% and 54% advantage.)

Over the last 26 elections (going back to Wilson's defeat of Hughes in 1916), there have been 9 elections where the difference in the popular vote was less than 5%, so that we find it meaningful to talk about a candidate's electoral advantage. Ranking them by the winner's advantage, those elections are:

| Year | Winner | Electoral Advantage |
| --- | --- | --- |
| 2016 | Trump | 2.85% |
| 1968 | Nixon | 1.58% |
| 2012 | Obama | 1.51% |
| 2000 | Bush | 0.52% |
| 1960 | Kennedy | 0.35% |
| 2004 | Bush | -0.35% |
| 1976 | Carter | -0.38% |
| 1916 | Wilson | -2.74% |
| 1948 | Truman | -4.04% |

**We observe the following:**

• Donald Trump had the best electoral advantage of any victor.
• Truman's surprise victory in 1948 is all the more impressive given that he overcame the worst electoral disadvantage.
• In these elections, the Republican candidate averaged a 1.10% electoral advantage.

This last point is worth further investigation. It is likely a combination of Republicans tending to do better in rural states (which tend to have more electors relative to their size) and Democratic candidates running up the score in more populous urban states (which helps with the popular vote, but not with the Electoral College).

# Section Three
# The Future of the Electoral College

# 9

## If the Electoral College Can Contradict the Popular Vote Sometimes, Why Would It Be Wrong for Them To Do It Every Single Time?*

Jack Russell Weinstein

In my role as a public philosopher, I received a question from one of my blog readers asking about the independence of the Electoral College.[1] The person wrote:

> Long before the election, my class was discussing the Electoral College, and one student opined that it should be kept because the popular vote doesn't accord with the electoral vote only some of the time. This got me thinking, "Would we find it acceptable if the popular vote never matched the electoral vote?" It would seem that whatever makes it acceptable to have the popular vote not match the electoral vote in some instances, would also make such an outcome acceptable in every instance. Or, conversely, whatever makes it unacceptable to have the popular vote not match the electoral vote in every instance, would also make such an outcome unacceptable in each instance. But perhaps I'm missing something, so I thought I'd see what you have to say in regard to the argumentation.

To put the question another way: if it is okay for the Electoral College to contradict the popular vote once in a while, why isn't it okay

* A version of this essay appeared as Jack Russell Weinstein, "If the Electoral College can contradict the popular vote sometimes, why would it be wrong for them to do it every single time?" *PQED: Philosophical Questions Every Day* (blog), November 28, 2016, http://www.pqed.org/2016/11/if-electoral-college-can-contradict.html

for it to do so all the time? How can opposing the popular vote be right only some of the time?

This is a good, philosophically interesting, and relevant question. To answer it, we first have to ask why we have an Electoral College in the first place, although, surprisingly, there isn't a consensus on this basic fact.

One theory is that the Electoral College was intended to give an equalizing voice to a region of slaveholders with a smaller white population. There is some evidence for this. James Madison himself seemed concerned that "the right of suffrage was much more diffusive in the Northern than the Southern States; and the latter could have no influence in the election on the score of Negroes" (Madison Debates, July 19, 1787).[2] In other words, since there were more Northern than Southern voters, without the Electoral College, the South would not be able to protect its right to maintain slaves.

Some cite Madison's argument as a case against the very legitimacy of the Electoral College itself, but such a critique isn't persuasive. It runs afoul of the Genetic Fallacy, the observation that the truth or validity of a conclusion does not depend on its history or origin. Why the Electoral College came into being is irrelevant to its current purpose. GPS was invented for the military, yet many peace activists still use it. Adolf Hitler designed the Volkswagen Beetle (although one scholar argues that Hitler stole it from a Jewish engineer),[3] yet people who drive them do not necessary subscribe to his fascist philosophy. Similarly, just because the Electoral College may have been in support of slavery at one time does not mean it is now.

In fact, the real remedy for the Southern states' disproportionately small influence was the Three-Fifths Compromise found in Article 1 of the U.S. Constitution. Also proposed at 1787 con-

---

[1] *PQED: Philosophical Questions Every Day* (blog) http://www.pqed.org/
[2] James Madison, "July 19, 1787," in *Notes of debates in the Federal Convention of 1787*. See Documents section.
[3] Paul Schilperoord, *The Extraordinary Life of Josef Ganz: The Jewish Engineer Behind Hitler's Volkswagen*. (New York : RVP Publishers, 2012).

stitutional convention, this clause declared that slaves should be counted as three-fifths of a freeperson for voting and taxation.

The Compromise is frequently and understandably touted as a philosophical synecdoche of American racism. But it's purpose was not to reduce the humanity of the slave to less than one as it is usually described; it was to *give* a slave some electoral power in the first place, and, by extension, the electoral power of the South.

Naturally, I do not mean to suggest that the compromise is not racist. It is. Slaves did not actually vote, slaveholders simply justified their additional electoral power on the backs of slaves using the Electoral College to consolidate their power. My point is simply that people tend not to understand its origins, giving credence, yet again, to the Genetic Fallacy, and making slavery less important to *today's* debate about the Electoral College. Once slavery was abolished in 1865 and the Three-Fifths Compromise rendered obsolete, this aspect of the Electoral College remained historically important but functionally irrelevant.

Another popular justification for the Electoral College also stems from the Madison debate: that it is a kind of "affirmative action" for rural voters. Given the different population densities of urban and agricultural regions, the Electors are supposed to equalize the power of voters across the country. This is the same sort of justification the framers used when apportioning two Senators per state regardless of their size, while basing the number of Representatives in the House on population. Without it, many claim, urban populations would determine all national elections.

This notion of the Electoral College emphasizes the lack of direct democracy in the Federal system. It echoes the Three-Fifths Compromise in that it holds that for votes to be equal, they need not be identical. Equality necessitates proportional, not uniform, representation.

But there is a problem with continuing to justify the Electoral College on these grounds. First, it assumes that rural voters have inherently different interests than urban voters, a generalization that simply doesn't hold. Political positions must be evaluated on a case-by-case basis, there is no reason to think that living in the country or the city would affect one's position on international relations, abortion, interstate commerce, net neutrality, or the vast majority of issues that concern government policies. It may affect one's position on agricultural issues, but even there, farmers disagree on ethanol, genetically modified seeding, and the importance of monoculture farming, to name just a few controversies.

People also tend to assume that rural voters are necessarily more conservative than urban voters, but this is simply not the case. For many decades, Appalachia was a Democratic stronghold. It isn't anymore; it changed. But that just proves my point. And while much has been made of the "traditional" family farm, there are few populations that are more embracing of technological change and government subsidies, and more suspicious of school choice than small farmers. ("Vouchers" and charter schools are untenable in rural areas where many towns share a single school.) The rural and urban electorate can simply not be cleanly divided into conservative and liberal, no matter how much lip service is given to the so-called "real America."

Regardless of all of these considerations, if increased representation of the rural is the reason for the Electoral College, then it simply failed to do its job in 2016. It did not magnify the agricultural voice; it increased the influence of the suburbs instead. As Joel Kotkin and Wendell Cox summarize in Forbes magazine, it wasn't alleged rural racism that rocketed Trump to power, it was the suburban five-point lead, a three-point increase from Romney in 2012.[4]

To summarize: if slavery is the reason for the Electoral College, we can't answer the reader's question at all and if voter equity is the reason, then all we have learned is that the Electoral College has failed. We do not yet know whether there is a moral difference between the college opposing the popular vote sometimes and it differing all the time.

---

[4] Joel Kotkin and Wendell Cox, "It Wasn't Rural 'Hicks' Who Elected Trump: The Suburbs Were -- And Will Remain -- The Real Battleground," Forbes. November 22, 2016. Accessed on December 31, 2016. http://www.forbes.com/sites/joelkotkin/2016/11/22/donald-trump-clinton-rural-suburbs/

However, the answer to the reader's question can be found, I think, in what I have always understood as the true purpose of the Electoral College: to be an educated body in the face of an uneducated public. From Plato onward, one of the most trenchant criticisms of democracy has been that public policy is simply too complex for the average person to understand. One needs both special training in political reasoning, the argument asserts, as well as to be able to emancipate oneself from private interest to qualify as enlightened voter.

This is the tradition that Hamilton calls upon in *Federalist* No. 68 when he wrote: "electors should be men most capable of analyzing the qualities adapted to the station and acting under circumstances favorable to deliberation…[they would be] most likely to have the information and discernment" required to choose the president.[5] Ultimately, he argued, the presidency should be determined by the most *qualified* voter, not by people who vote simply because they are *eligible*.

What might have Hamilton meant by these comments and how does this change the role of the Electoral College? There are, it seems to me, two possible interpretations—and two possible answers to our main question—depending on whether this layer of qualified electors are to be regarded as insurance or as a representative body.

Let's begin with the first interpretation, that is, that the job of the Electoral College is to be a last-ditch effort to protect the country from a demagogue who fools the public into voting for him or her. If this is the case, then the Electoral College should be regarded as an insurance policy and, as with all insurance, we hope never to have to use it. We buy insurance hoping to waste our money.

Under this interpretation, if the Electoral College contradicts the popular vote with good reason, we should celebrate their choice. However, if it does so under conditions different than its prescribed safeguard, if, for example, the candidate is not dangerous or a demagogue, but simply won because of the vicissitudes of

---

[5] James Madison, *Federalist* No.68, in *The Federalist Papers*. See Documents section.

electoral politics, then such a decision is to be deplored and the presidency is illegitimate. This illegitimacy is, however, something we have to put up with to preserve the protection we might some-day need. In such a case, a president who did not win the popular vote is the "price we pay" for the Electoral College.

In other words, if we consider the Electoral College as an insurance policy against demagoguery, the justification for the Electoral College is utilitarian. We are willing to accept some bad stuff for the greater good. An occasional disagreement between it and the popular vote can be justified, but continual disagreement cannot.

My personal feeling, by the way, is that this is the true purpose of the Electoral College. Since it did not protect us from Trump, it will never protect us from anyone and can no longer be justified. Even more so, since one of Hamilton's specific concerns was that the vote might be corrupted by "foreign powers to gain an improper ascendant in our councils," it failed in its very specific mandate.[6] As a preponderance of evidence has shown, Russia significantly influenced the election, orchestrating a Clinton loss despite her popular-vote landslide. The Electors knew this but disregarded it, emphasizing that the Electoral College no longer plays its intended part as insurer. It has become, instead, a tool for partisan sidestepping of the popular vote.

The second possible interpretation of Hamilton's preference for educated electors over the general population leads to a deontological justification for the Electoral College—it builds on a principle that allows for no exception. It puts forth the idea of representative government in its strongest from, regarding electors themselves as agents akin to all of our officials, not simply protectors with narrow mandates whom we call upon in very specific situations.

If we regard Electors as representatives—if we see them like Congress members or as specialists who have more refined political senses than the layperson—then we have to think of the popular vote as only advisory rather than binding. In other words, when the general populace votes and expresses its will, the Electors ought

---

[6] Madison, *Federalist* No.68. See Documents section.

to consider it as only one of many factors, and then vote based on their personal (allegedly professional and educated) judgment. This may or may not assume their personal judgment is better, but it does regard their representative role as having more *authority* to choose the president than an average voter.

There are, incidentally, good and convincing fictional portrayals of this point of view. In an episode of *The West Wing* titled "The Lame Duck Congress," when faced with deciding whether to approve a nuclear treaty against the wishes of 82% of the voters, the fictional President Bartlett says:

> Can I tell you something, honestly? This is one of those situations where I couldn't give a damn what the people think. The complexities of a global arms treaty, the technological, the military, the diplomatic nuances, it's staggering, Toby. 82% of the people cannot possibly be expected to reach an informed decision.

Bartlett's point is taken significantly farther by President Andrew Shepherd, in the movie *The American President*:

> **Lewis Rothschild**: ...People want leadership, Mr. President, and in the absence of genuine leadership, they'll listen to anyone who steps up to the microphone. They want leadership. They're so thirsty for it they'll crawl through the desert toward a mirage, and when they discover there's no water, they'll drink the sand.
>
> **President Andrew Shepherd**: Lewis, we've had presidents who were beloved, who couldn't find a coherent sentence with two hands and a flashlight. People don't drink the sand because they're thirsty. They drink the sand because they don't know the difference.

If this point of view is correct and if the American population is simply not educated enough to make good democratic decisions, then the popular vote is simply advisory to the Electoral College rather than binding. And, if this is the case, the College's decision is, by definition, always right. It and only it, has the job of choosing our president. In such an interpretation of Hamilton's words, there is no such thing as an electoral vote that contradicts the popular vote, just one that considered it and moved on.

One final observation: differing attitudes about voter knowledge is a point of contention in the debate between John Locke and Jean Jacques Rousseau, the patron saints of American and French democracy, respectively. The role of individual perspective marks a dividing line between the American notion that people's beliefs about their own interest is more important than their generalized knowledge, and the French democratic model, which assumes that personal interest is secondary to collective understanding, or the Republic's interests. Hamilton's view of the Electoral College as permanent representative seems to fit more with the French model than the American one, suggesting, yet again, that the Electoral College is inconsistent with American democratic values. It seems to me that the given all we have discussed, the only viable justification for the Electoral College is one based on its role as insurance against demagoguery and, as we have seen, it has failed in its role. Certainly, this conclusion is based in part on my own political leanings, but that doesn't make it wrong. Perspective and bias are not the same thing.

Nevertheless, to sum up my rather lengthy answer to the reader's question: if the Electoral College is insurance, then we have to put up with a couple unjustified conflicts in order to protect ourselves against potential serious dangers. In such a case, the Electoral College must agree with the popular vote in most but not all instances, and when it doesn't, we have to regard it as a necessary evil.

But if the Electoral College plays a representative role and the general popular vote is advisory, then it is theoretically possible for the Electoral College to disagree with the majority every single time and still be legitimate. In this case, the popular vote will always be secondary to the judgment of its representatives. Or, as President Bartlett puts it immediately after his comment above: "…we forget sometimes, in all the talk about democracy, we forget it's not a democracy, it's a republic. People don't make the decisions, they choose the people who make the decisions. Could they do a better job choosing? Yeah. But when you consider the alternatives,…"

As is hopefully evident, the reader's question goes to the heart of the American experiment. Are we a democracy or a republic, and if we are one or the other, is it what we were supposed to be or just what we ended up as? The Genetic Fallacy makes original intent a less powerful argument for any constitutional interpretation, but it doesn't make it less interesting. Whatever damages the Electoral College may or may not have inflicted this time around, the fact that it has given us an opportunity to reflect on the nature of democracy is itself a gift worth celebrating.

# 10

## Electoral College is Fixable; Senate is Not.

Mark Trahant

The Electoral College was a huge mistake. It's anti-democratic. It's 18th century machinery designed to elect a government despite deep philosophical differences between states, regions and cities. And, in a digital economy, the mechanics makes no sense.

But the funny thing is: The Electoral College is fixable.

If votes were counted proportionally, instead of winner-take-call, the results would be a lot closer to the popular will and still account for regional differences in thinking. (This reform would not require a Constitutional amendment, but all 50 states would have to agree.)

Indeed the Electoral College gets the attention for being un-democratic when there are other issues in the American version of democracy that cry out for real reform.

Consider the notion of requiring a super-majority in the Senate (a filibuster-proof 60 votes). The Senate elects two members from each state. So California's 36 million citizens get two votes – exactly the same as Wyoming's 532,000 people. And the super-majority makes matters worse because senators representing a tiny slice of the population can block legislation that most Americans favor.

The Senate has a unique history and in that favorite argument used by so many, "we have always done it that way." But let's be clear about this, the structure of the Senate does not represent democratic values. Why does this matter? Especially when it's worked for more than two centuries?

The Senate ceased its claim to democracy in 1920 when the census showed that the United States had become an urban nation.

A century ago this did not matter because the values and priorities were largely the same; the opposite is true now. The greatest divide in our politics stems from this rural, urban split on issues ranging from natural resource extraction to climate change. Yet the Senate skews rural dramatically. It only takes 17 percent of the country to elect a majority in the Senate (and that's not even including the additional ten votes required for a supermajority.)

The House is not particularly democratic either. The United States is one of the few countries in the world that clings to a district system that can be manipulated by a political party. Districts are designed to favor incumbents or the party in power. In other countries, proportional representation insures that all constituent groups are represented in body politic. In a district system, however, the other party is often shut out from all elective offices in a state.

Could there be reform without a new Constitution? Perhaps. States could create multiple congressional districts. And California could split into two, three or even four states, to even out the Senate a bit. We need more representation, not less. So I'd like to see a Senate the size of the House now and a people House of Representatives that was significantly larger in order to accommodate more points of view.

Democratic reform is critical when the U.S. preaches it as a value to the rest of the world. That means system reform, well beyond a quick fix to the Electoral College. And, who knows? After reform a proportional Electoral College could actually work. Even in a digital century.

# 11

## Long Habits and Legitimacy

Mark Stephen Jendrysik

"A long habit of not thinking a thing wrong, gives it a superficial appearance of being right, and raises at first a formidable outcry in defense of custom." When Thomas Paine said this in *Common Sense* (1776) he was speaking about monarchy, but he could have been saying it about the Electoral College (EC).[1] The EC might once have had a purpose, and it can be argued that the EC was necessary at the beginning of the republic to overcome the basic problems of time and space that made rapid communication of electoral results across a continent-spanning nation difficult if not impossible.[2] This constitutional feature was designed for a very different time.

Like other features of the United States Constitution such as state equality in the Senate, the EC is now an ossified remnant of a distant past that creates a crisis of political legitimacy every time the EC fails to ratify the popular vote. While this has only happened four times in the history of the country (1876, 1888, 2000 and 2016), current demographic and political division make it possible this outcome might become a regular event. If elections are repeatedly resolved in the EC to the detriment of popular majorities, possibly numbering in the millions, America will face a crisis of legitimacy. After all, why should the election of the president be

---

[1] T. Paine, *Common Sense*. Philadelphia: Printed. And sold by W . and T. Bradford [1776]). Accessed on December 31, 2016. http://xroads.virginia.edu/~hyper/Paine/common.html

[2] It generally took at least two weeks to travel from New York to Charleston, South Carolina in 1800.

the only election where the majority (or plurality) does not determine the winner?[3]

Every argument in favor of the EC is made mindlessly, or in bad faith, or to cover up less than savory ideas. To co-opt George Orwell, the EC "can indeed be defended, but only by arguments which are too brutal for most people to face."[4] Mindless defenses of the EC pop up every four years. Repeatedly saying "We are a republic not a democracy" is not an argument, it is an incantation. Claiming the EC is a feature of state sovereignty ignores that fact that the states are not actually sovereign. Saying "that's how the Founders set it up, and they were greater men than we are" infantilizes those of us alive today. Such thinking makes us children, forced to forever obey the Framers, without volition or reason of our own. To paraphrase Paine, the Founders might as well have declared themselves immortal, since we now have no choice but to follow their will.[5]

Bad faith arguments in support of the EC are easy to find. Donald Trump's complaints about the EC turned to praise once he discovered it was working in his favor. We can also note people who say we can just amend the Constitution to get rid of the EC, while knowing full well that will never happen. Or we can consider the arguments of people in small states whose votes count for more than the voters of more populous states. Defending a weighted vote system requires a set of rather dubious and ultimately disturbing assumptions.[6] For example, saying that the EC protects the interests of rural areas against urban ones, suggests that some voters votes should have a greater weight. After all, "Real Americans ™"

---

[3] In a similar sense, state equality in the Senate poses serious questions of legitimacy as well. Currently somewhat less the 15% of the population controls over half the seats in the Senate, a trend which will only grow more extreme.

[4] G. Orwell, "Politics and the English Language," *Horizon* Vol. 13, No. 76. (April 1946), 261.

[5] See T. Paine, *Rights of Man* (London: Joseph Johnson, 1791) for a discussion of the absurdity of the idea that the dead can constrain the living.

[6] Or, maybe you believe that empty space should be allowed to vote.

are the honest sons of the soil, not untrustworthy city slickers. As Michael Barone notoriously claimed, the EC protects the country from the rule of the voters of California, who, as we all know, don't represent or support real American values.[7] And so it is only just that their votes count for less in the EC.

The United States Constitution is an admirable document. But parts of it can be compared to a petrified forest, once alive and vibrant, now merely existing. Even worse, parts of it, in particular the EC, are like vestigial organs. Like the appendix, the EC is mostly harmless and unnoticed. But every once in a while, the EC reminds us of its existence and threatens the health and safety of the Republic. In a democracy elections decided by less than a majority are, on their face, illegitimate.[8] Quite simply, choosing the single most important office in the world through anti-democratic methods leaves a ticking time bomb of disaster at the heart of our political system.

---

[7] Michael Barone, "Ditching the Electoral College" *Washington Examiner*, December 4, 2016. Accessed December 31, 2016. http://www. washingtonexaminer.com/ditching-electoral-college-would-allow-california-to-impose-imperial-rule-on-a-colonial-america/article/2608766 The key paragraph: "California's 21st century veer to the left makes it a live issue again. In a popular vote system, the voters of this geographically distant and culturally distinct state, whose contempt for heartland Christians resembles imperial London's disdain for the 'lesser breeds' it governed, could impose something like colonial rule over the rest of the nation. Sounds exactly like what the Framers strove to prevent."
[8] There are over 500,000 elected officials in the United States. All of them, except the president are chosen by majority or plurality elections. David Nir, "Just how many elected officials are there in the United States? The answer is mind-blowing," *Daily Kos*. March 29, 2015. Accessed on December 31, 2016. http://www.dailykos.com/story/2015/3/29/1372225/-Just-how-many-elected-officials-are-there-in-the-United-States-The-answer-is-mind-blowing

# 12

## In Defense of the Electoral College[*]

Allen Guelzo and James H. Hulme

There is hardly anything in the Constitution harder to explain, or easier to misunderstand, than the Electoral College. And when a presidential election hands the palm to a candidate who comes in second in the popular vote but first in the Electoral College tally, something deep in our democratic viscera balks and asks why the Electoral College shouldn't be dumped as a useless relic of 18th century white, gentry privilege.

Actually, there have been only five occasions when a closely divided popular vote and the electoral vote have failed to point in the same direction. No matter. After last week's results, we're hearing a litany of complaints: the Electoral College is undemocratic, the Electoral College is unnecessary, the Electoral College was invented to protect slavery — and the demand to push it down the memory hole.

All of which is strange because the Electoral College is at the core of our system of federalism. The Founders who sat in the 1787 Constitutional Convention lavished an extraordinary amount of argument on the Electoral College, and it was by no means one-sided. The great Pennsylvania jurist James Wilson believed that "if we are to establish a national Government," the president should be chosen by a direct, national vote of the people. But wise old Roger Sherman of Connecticut replied that the president ought to be elected by Congress, since he feared that direct election of presidents by the people would lead to the creation of a

---

[*]A version of this essay appeared as Allen Guelzo and James Hulme, "In defense of the Electoral College," *PostEverything* (blog), *The Washington Post*, November 15, 2016, http://www.washingtonpost.com/postevery-thing/wp/2016/11/15/in-defense-of-the-electoral-college/

monarchy. "An independence of the Executive [from] the supreme Legislature, was in his opinion the very essence of tyranny if there was any such thing." Sherman was not trying to undermine the popular will, but to keep it from being distorted by a president who mistook popular election as a mandate for dictatorship.

Quarrels like this flared all through the convention, until, at almost the last minute, James Madison "took out a Pen and Paper, and sketched out a mode of Electing the President" by a "college" of "Electors ... chosen by those of the people in each State, who shall have the Qualifications requisite."

The Founders also designed the operation of the Electoral College with unusual care. The portion of Article 2, Section 1, describing the Electoral College is longer and descends to more detail than any other single issue the Constitution addresses. More than the federal judiciary — more than the war powers — more than taxation and representation. It prescribes in precise detail how "Each State shall appoint ... a Number of Electors, equal to the whole Number of Senators and Representatives to which the State may be entitled in the Congress"; how these electors "shall vote by Ballot" for a president and vice president; how they "shall sign and certify, and transmit sealed to the Seat of the Government of the United States, directed to the President of the Senate" the results of their balloting; how a tie vote must be resolved; what schedule the balloting should follow; and on and on.

Above all, the Electoral College had nothing to do with slavery. Some historians have branded the Electoral College this way because each state's electoral votes are based on that "whole Number of Senators and Representatives" from each State, and in 1787 the number of those representatives was calculated on the basis of the infamous three-fifths clause. But the Electoral College merely reflected the numbers, not any bias about slavery (and in any case, the three-fifths clause was not quite as proslavery a compromise as it seems, since Southern slaveholders wanted their slaves counted as five-fifths for determining representation in Congress, and had to settle for a whittled-down fraction). As much as the abolitionists before the Civil War liked to talk about the "proslavery Constitution," this was more of a rhetorical posture than a serious historical argument. And the simple fact remains, from the record of the Constitutional Convention's proceedings (James Madison's famous Notes), that the discussions of the Electoral College and the method of electing a president never occur in the context of any of the convention's two climactic debates over slavery.

If anything, it was the Electoral College that made it possible to end slavery, since Abraham Lincoln earned only 39 percent of the popular vote in the election of 1860, but won a crushing victory in the Electoral College. This, in large measure, was why Southern slaveholders stampeded to secession in 1860-61. They could do the numbers as well as anyone, and realized that the Electoral College would only produce more anti-slavery Northern presidents.

Yet, even on those terms, it is hard for Americans to escape the uncomfortable sense that, by inserting an extra layer of "electors" between the people and the president, the Electoral College is something less than democratic. But even if we are a democratic nation, that is not all we are. The Constitution also makes us a federal union, and the Electoral College is pre-eminently both the symbol and a practical implementation of that federalism.

The states of the union existed before the Constitution, and in a practical sense, existed long before the revolution. Nothing guaranteed that, in 1776, the states would all act together, and nothing that guaranteed that after the Revolution they might not go their separate and quarrelsome ways, much like the German states of the 18th century or the South American republics in the 19th century. The genius of the Constitutional Convention was its ability to entice the American states into a "more perfect union." But it was still a union of states, and we probably wouldn't have had a constitution or a country at all unless the route we took was federalism.

The Electoral College was an integral part of that federal plan. It made a place for the states as well as the people in electing the president by giving them a say at different points in a federal process and preventing big-city populations from dominating the election of a president.

Abolishing the Electoral College now might satisfy an irritated yearning for direct democracy, but it would also mean dismantling federalism. After that, there would be no sense in having a Senate (which, after all, represents the interests of the states), and further along, no sense even in having states, except as administrative departments of the central government. Those who wish to abolish the Electoral College ought to go the distance, and do away with the entire federal system and perhaps even retire the Constitution, since the federalism it was designed to embody would have disappeared.

None of that, ironically, is liable to produce a more democratic election system. There are plenty of democracies, like Great Britain, where no one ever votes directly for a head of the government. But more important, the Electoral College actually keeps presidential elections from going undemocratically awry because it makes unlikely the possibility that third-party candidates will garner enough votes to make it onto the electoral scoreboard.

Without the Electoral College, there would be no effective brake on the number of "viable" presidential candidates. Abolish it, and it would not be difficult to imagine a scenario where, in a field of a dozen micro-candidates, the "winner" only needs 10 percent of the vote, and represents less than 5 percent of the electorate. And presidents elected with smaller and smaller pluralities will only aggravate the sense that an elected president is governing without a real electoral mandate.

The Electoral College has been a major, even if poorly comprehended, mechanism for stability in a democracy, something which democracies are sometimes too flighty to appreciate. It may appear inefficient. But the Founders were not interested in efficiency; they were interested in securing "the blessings of liberty." The Electoral College is, in the end, not a bad device for securing that.

# 13

## Electoral College Alternatives: Tradeoffs

Benjamin J. Kassow

Forty-eight states use a popular vote method to allocate electoral votes (two states, Nebraska and Maine, use a partially congressional-district based allocation for the electoral votes in those states). One of the key controversies regarding the Electoral College has been the degree to which the Electoral College is perceived by some to be "anti-democratic" in that people argue that the Electoral College does not reflect the "will of the people." To me, as is often the case, the key thought is thinking about the Electoral College as it currently exists and other possible electoral systems for the presidency in terms of a series of tradeoffs.

What might these tradeoffs look like? First, do we want a system that directly reflects the will of the largest plurality of Americans, the majority (50+%) of voting Americans, or one that reflects some level of dispersion and geographic viability throughout a variety of regions in the country? Secondly, depending on what we prioritize as a country, what system might we want that would reflect these priorities? Thirdly, do most Americans want the Electoral College to change? Finally, if many Americans want to reform the Electoral College, what tradeoffs would we want to make to ensure that people feel that their vote counts?

One first question is how the Electoral College could be changed, from a logistical perspective. On first glance, eliminating (or strongly modifying) the Electoral College looks daunting. At a most basic level, the Constitution must be amended, which of course, is exceedingly difficult. While other approaches are possible to use (changing electoral laws in the states, for instance, which decide how to allocate Electoral College votes), questions remain as to what might be the most feasible method to do so. Still, many attempts to change the Electoral College certainly exist in American history, although only one has really been fundamental in terms of changing the Electoral College allocation proposal in a serious way: the Bayh-Celler (H.R. J. Res. 681) Amendment (1969) proposal. The intractability of eliminating or massively changing the Electoral College is reflected in the relatively few major attempts at the federal level since the Civil War. Additionally, there are still substantial questions as to what tradeoffs we might want to have as a country, assuming a different approach from what we have now.

The second approach: changing state legislation as to how states distribute their Electoral College votes. While this is more practical, it also raises other potential issues of inequity among states, and how much your vote may count for president being in one state versus another. Unless somehow all states could change concurrently, simply changing a state or two would likely result in other problems, including substantial differences in how states award electors. This could lead to the potential for large inequities among states as to how people's votes actually count in presidential elections. From a Constitutional standpoint, specifically with regards to the Equal Protection Clause, this may prove problematic (see *Bush v Gore*, 531 U.S. 98, [2000]), and may lead to other concerns about how individual's votes are counted (i.e., if it varies dramatically among states).

Even if a majority of United States citizens approves reforming the Electoral College, another question of practicality also rears its head. If we open the Electoral College "Pandora's box," then what problems might we have with any other potential solution? Certainly, if we were to have a national popular vote, there would be strong criticisms by many that the will of states would be taken away. Similarly, if we were to adopt a different system, would that help to solve the problems that those who criticize the Electoral College level at the College? While it might, depending on the solution chosen, a host of other questions would also arise.

So, what could potentially be an alternative to the Electoral College, as it currently stands? President Nixon himself, in 1969, proposed replacing the Electoral College with a national popular-vote based system that would simply award the presidential candidate with the highest percentage of the popular vote the presidency. One tool in this proposal would have prevented a candidate with a very small percentage of the popular vote from leading, which would be a mandatory runoff election between the top two candidates if no candidate exceeded 40% of the popular vote. But what tradeoff would a system like this have? The fate of the Bayh-Celler amendment, although it is only one case, is perhaps quite instructive as to the various tradeoffs involved with altering how the Electoral College functions, at the federal level. While the amendment passed with bipartisan support through the House of Representatives, it was successfully filibustered in the Senate, because it would damage the ability of smaller states to influence the outcome of United States presidential elections in the future. So, as I have already mentioned, the constant tradeoff is in terms of how to distribute voting power to choose the president: should it be distributed to individuals as one person in the entire United States, or distributed to individuals as part of an individual state *within* the United States?

In closing, thinking about the Electoral College, regardless of whether we may be in favor of it, opposed to it, or decidedly neutral, requires us to consider a series of tradeoffs. Do we want a political system that encourages political candidates to have majorities of geographic regions within the United States, or one that encourage presidential candidates to win the most votes more generally? Which system better reflects the will of the people? In any case, when thinking about whether we approve of the Electoral College as is or whether/how we may wish to alter it, it is crucial to examine any tradeoffs we might be making if we were to change it.

# Section Four
# Teaching the Electoral College

# 14

## "Empathy for the Unicorn": Teaching About the Electoral College

Brad Austin

I approach the topic of "teaching the electoral college" from two different, if related, perspectives.[1] The first is that of an historian trained in modern American history, someone who teaches about the disputed elections of 1876 and 2000 and who notes how a few thousand votes in specific states would have denied John F. Kennedy the presidency in 1960 and given the nation President Nixon ahead of schedule. Like most teachers, I address the basic "rules of the game" of the Electoral College and explain how a candidate can attract more popular support than his (and now, her) opposition but still lose the election. Other essays in this volume offer teachers and other interested citizens the historical contexts they need to teach the mechanics and specific consequences of the Electoral College and those elections.

My second perspective is that of someone who trains future high and middle school history teachers and who spends most of my "methods of teaching history" course encouraging my students to make their own classes about more than the mere memorization of names, dates, treaties, and battles. As someone who emphasizes the importance of teaching historical thinking skills (close reading of sources, chronological thinking, determining causation, identi-

---

[1] Oddly enough, I discussed the relationship between North Dakota and the Electoral College with my Massachusetts university students during a wide-ranging conversation on the day after the election. If I recall correctly, my remark was something along the lines of "One of the consequences of the electoral college is that individual North Dakota voters have a lot more power than we do in presidential elections."

fying perspectives, etc.), I embrace the opportunities that studying the Electoral College provides to teachers who want to challenge their students' assumptions and to give them materials and questions that push them to formulate arguments and to think for themselves.

Sam Wineburg, in his path-breaking *Historical Thinking and Other Unnatural Acts*, recounts the story of Marco Polo and the world's ugliest unicorns.[2] As Wineburg explains, during his travels, Polo came across an animal with a head "like a wild Boar" and a short, stubby horn. Obviously, it was a unicorn. Polo concluded that this animal was "a passing ugly beast to look upon, and is not in the least like that which our stories tell of as being caught in the lap of a virgin; in fact, 'tis altogether different from what we fancied."[3] Modern readers, of course, recognize that Polo was describing a rhinoceros, not a unicorn, even if they might concede that virgins (and non-virgins alike) might be wise to avoid having one sit on their laps.

I include this story not because I find it intrinsically interesting (although I do), but because I second Wineburg's call for history instructors to use their lessons and their classes to enhance their students' capacities for empathy, for understanding how others perceive and experience the world. This story demonstrates how even very worldly, learned people are often inclined to consider new information and evidence within the confines of existing belief systems and paradigms for understanding the world. Put differently, we are too often blinded by what we "know" to recognize what we see.

After the 2016 presidential election results proved pundits to be spectacularly wrong, many commentators pointed to Americans' increasing inclination to avoid exposure to conflicting ideas and evidence as a reason for the surprise many felt when the out-

---

[2] Sam Wineburg, *Historical Thinking and Other Unnatural Acts: Charting the Future of Teaching the Past* (Temple University Press, 2011), 24.
[3] Marco Polo, *The Travels of Marco Polo: The Complete Yule-Cordier Edition* Dover Publications, 1993), 285.

come became clear. The causes of our current inability to agree on basic facts or the authority of experts will probably spawn a thousands dissertations and keep political scientists and sociologists employed for a generation, but it is not the focus of this essay. Our current situation, in fact, reminds us of the obligation history teachers have to prepare students for the demands of civic life, and teaching the Electoral College offers multiple opportunities for us to fulfill that obligation.

Teaching about the history of the Electoral College, and the ideologies and assumptions that led to its creation, allows instructors to challenge their students to see something new (a rhino) instead of seeing just another unicorn, if an ugly one. If our students are going to develop the ability to understand and appreciate different perspectives and viewpoints, then studying history is a great place to practice that skill. Specifically, it is vital that our students realize that "they" (the founding generation) did not think like "us." Heck, "they" didn't even think like each other, a fact that explains the emergence of Federalist and Anti-Federalist camps before the ratification of the Constitution and the almost immediate evolution of political factions into parties after the new government was formed. These divisions and disagreements present us with an abundance of opportunities for our students to explore how particular experiences (the Revolution, opposition to George III, Articles of Confederation, etc.), regional perspectives (coastal, in-land, North, South, small state, large state, etc.), economic situation (merchant, farmer, plantation owner, tradesman, enslaved person, etc.) led to different conclusions about the desirability of the new government and, especially, its purposefully convoluted and anti-democratic way of choosing a chief executive. In short, a close look at the intellectual roots of the Electoral College challenges students to understand how and why our "Founding Fathers" held vastly different opinions about the desirability of this system for selecting a president and to consider the roots of those disagreements.

Teachers looking for specific ways to do this need only to consult the Documents section of this volume to find abundant primary sources that can help them accomplish their pedagogical goals. For example, if teachers want to illustrate the wide variety of options considered by the delegates to the Constitutional Convention, then they can ask their students to read (and perhaps translate to 21st-century language) James Madison's notes on "Debates Concerning the Method of Selecting the Executive," especially those from June 1st and September 4th. The notes on June 1st illustrate some of the options initially considered (direct election, Congressional choice, Senate choice, etc.), and the September 4th notes document the ways that several leaders argued over the proposed Electoral College plan, with Governeur Morris offering a succinct six-part defense of the plan in response to some pointed criticism. While teachers would be well served to familiarize themselves with the rest of the debate, these two sections alone give students enough to see how personal experiences, others' histories, and political philosophies led delegates to very different conclusions about the Electoral College.

Students will also be interested to see that the text of the Constitution reflects the delegates' desires to cede considerable power to the states and their legislature. As one can see in Documents section, Article II, Section 1 of the Constitution reads, in part, "Each State shall appoint, in such manner as the Legislature may direct, a number of electors, equal to the whole number of Senators and Representatives to which the State may be entitled in the Congress: but no Senator or Representative, or person holding an office of trust or profit under the United States, shall be appointed an elector." Teachers can ask students to create an imaginative and comprehensive list of different ways those states could have chosen their electors, given only these instructions, and to consider the says these options would have empowered different groups.

Given the popularity of the Broadway musical based on his life, Alexander Hamilton's involvement in the debate might attract the attention of students. While he participated in the convention debates, Hamilton's most important contributions to our understanding of the purpose of the Electoral College are found in his essay, *Federalist* No. 68, available in the Documents section.

Here, Hamilton notes that the Electoral College might be the one part of the Constitution that had not yet sparked great discussion, something he credited to the fact "that if the manner of [selecting the president] be not perfect, it is at least excellent. It unites in an eminent degree all the advantages, the union of which was to be wished for." The next several paragraphs outlines those advantages for readers, and they do so in language that is accessible to students who want to see the best case Hamilton could make for the Electoral College. Teachers might want to know if their 21st century students agree with Hamilton about the value of these elements of the Electoral College.

If they have their students read Hamilton's thoughts, then teachers might also want to introduce their students to *Antifederalist* No. 72, in which Republicus questions the wisdom of using an Electoral College to choose an executive. In this essay (also available in the Documents section), the author offers an extended critique of this method:

> "I go now to Art. 2, Sec. 1, which vest the supreme continental executive power in a president -- in order to the choice of whom, the legislative body of each state is empowered to point out to their constituents some mode of choice, or (to save trouble) may choose themselves, a certain number of electors, who shall meet in their respective states, and vote by ballot, for two persons, one of whom, at least, shall not be an inhabitant of the same state with themselves. Or in other words, they shall vote for two, one or both of whom they know nothing of...
>
> Is it then become necessary, that a free people should first resign their right of suffrage into other hands besides their own, and then, secondly, that they to whom they resign it should be compelled to choose men, whose persons, characters, manners, or principles they know nothing of? And, after all (excepting some such change as is not likely to happen twice in the same century) to intrust Congress with the final decision at last? Is it

necessary, is it rational, that the sacred rights of mankind should thus dwindle down to Electors of electors, and those again electors of other electors? This seems to be degrading them even below the prophetical curse denounced by the good old patriarch, on the offspring of his degenerate son: 'servant of servants'."

Given that there was clearly a public debate over the Constitution and its many provisions, teachers can seize the opportunity to put their students in the shoes of the partisans. In this case, in order to have their students understand some of the most important arguments for and against the Electoral College, teachers could have students use Madison's notes, Hamilton's *Federalist* No. 68, and the Anti-Federalist essay as their main sources for a classroom debate, with students being free to offer their own suggestions for choosing a president as well. This exercise would allow, but not require, students to research the biographies of the central figures and, among the more creative and theatrical students, it could lead to *Hamilton*-style "cabinet meeting" rap battles that draw on specific primary sources and present historically accurate arguments.

I'd like to conclude with a final note about how we can profitably talk about assumptions and the Electoral College in the classroom. It is worth noting (or leading our students to the realization), that however much they disagreed about the mechanics and desirability of the Electoral College, the participants in this debate shared some common assumptions about who should have the right to vote and to participate in the political process. As other essays in this volume point out, one of the purposes of the Electoral College was to protect the rights of slaveholders by giving them disproportionate political power, thanks in part to the Three-Fifths clause elsewhere in the Constitution. Students should note that almost no one in the late eighteenth century publically advocated for women's political rights and that Massachusetts's new constitution stripped voting rights from citizens who did not meet the new, higher property-owning threshold for voting. Moreover, in the early 1800s, New Jersey stripped women of the right to vote in that state, and several other states passed new laws denying African

Americans the right to the franchise that they have had previously enjoyed. Essentially, "the people" in the new republic had a different connotation than it does today. When we ask our students to think about why the Founders designed such a complicated, undemocratic system as the Electoral College, it is useful to broaden the discussion to include *all* of the assumptions they made about the trustworthiness of the American electorate and who should properly have their views represented in the new government.

# Documents

# Documents

To prepare for the Constitutional Convention, James Madison studied the governmental and legal histories of other societies, focusing in particular on why past confederacies had failed. Yet despite all this research, about a month before the convention began, Madison confessed to George Washington that he had "scarcely ventured" to fashion an opinion about the form and powers that a "National executive" might have under a new constitution. As it turned out, many of the longest-running disputes at the convention concerned the executive branch, and, as Madison later remarked, the "difficulty of finding an unexceptionable" method for electing the president was "deeply felt" by the delegates. Document 1 (The Constitutional Convention) illuminates the philosophical and political issues that shaped the delegates' debates about the executive branch, while Document 2 (Article II of the U.S. Constitution) showcases the method of election they ultimately chose. Document 3 (*Federalist Paper* No. 68) is Alexander Hamilton's famous defense of the so-called Electoral College, while Document 4 (*Anti-Federalist Paper* No. 68) and Document 5 (*Anti-Federalist Paper* No. 72) represent the Anti-Federalist critique of the system. The ratification of the Constitution was not the end of the story, however. The partisan battles of the 1790s soon prompted an overhauling of the Electoral College, as illustrated by Document 6 (the 12th Amendment to the U.S. Constitution) and Document 7 (Timothy Pickering's 1803 speech in favor of the 12th Amendment). Nevertheless, as shown by Document 8 (Madison's 1823 letter to George Hay), Madison continued to perceive defects in the electoral process, lamenting that many states had embraced winner-take-all systems for selecting presidential electors, and that each state was accorded one vote when presidential elections devolved to the House of Representatives. Finally, as evident in Document 9 (Madison's 1830 letter to James Hillhouse), over forty years after the Constitutional Convention, Madison remained "duly sensible to the evils incident to the existing" system for picking the president, and welcomed efforts to improve it. However, even with the system's shortcomings, Madison was confident that "it will be a rare case that the Presidential contest will not issue in a choice that will not discredit the Station, and not be acquiesced in by the unsuccessful party, foreseeing as it must do, the appeal to be again made at no very distant day, to the will of the Nation."

In addition to the documents provided in this volume, many useful resources concerning the Electoral College can be found on the web. Wikipedia, for example, has interesting charts showing how states picked presidential electors during the early American republic and how each state's allotment of electoral votes has changed over time (https://en.wikipedia.org/wiki/Electoral_College_(United_States)).). As was the case during the nation's initial years, the 1960s witnessed extensive debates about the Electoral College. One of the most striking episodes occurred in 1966 when Delaware filed suit against New York, charging that the latter's winner-take-all system for awarding electoral votes hurt the less populous states (https://www.scribd.com/document/331930037/Delaware-v-New-York-1966). Also noteworthy during this period was President Lyndon B. Johnson's 1966 speech in favor of reform, and comparable addresses in 1969 by Congressman Gerald Ford and President Richard Nixon, all three of which can be found here (http://archive.fairvote.org/index.php?page=2054). More recently, the supporters of the National Popular Vote Interstate Compact have attempted to effectively replace the Electoral College with a national popular vote (http://www.nationalpopularvote.com), but their prospects for success appear uncertain, since a 2016 Gallop poll showed support for the Electoral College to be at a fifty-year high (http://www.gallup.com/poll/198917/americans-support-electoral-college-rises-sharply.aspx).

# Document 1

# The Constitutional Convention

*Debates Concerning the Method of Selecting the Executive
(June 1 - September 6, 1787)*

**FRIDAY June 1, 1787**
**William Houston from Georgia took his seat.**

The Committee of the whole proceeded to Resolution 7. "that a national Executive be instituted, to be chosen by the national Legislature-for the term of ------ years &c to be ineligible thereafter, to possess the executive powers of Congress &c."

 **Mr. PINKNEY** was for a vigorous Executive but was afraid the Executive powers of the existing Congress might extend to peace & war &c., which would render the Executive a monarchy, of the worst kind, to wit an elective one.

 **Mr. WILSON** moved that the Executive consist of a single person.

 **Mr. C PINKNEY** seconded the motion, so as to read "that a National Ex. to consist of a single person, be instituted.

 A considerable pause ensuing and the Chairman asking if he should put the question, Docr. FRANKLIN observed that it was a point of great importance and wished that the gentlemen would deliver their sentiments on it before the question was put.

 **Mr. RUTLIDGE** animadverted on the shyness of gentlemen on this and other subjects. He said it looked as if they supposed themselves precluded by having frankly disclosed their opinions from afterwards changing them, which he did not take to be at all the case. He said he was for vesting the Executive power in a single person, tho' he was not for giving him the power of war and peace. A single man would feel the greatest responsibility and administer the public affairs best.

**Mr. SHERMAN** said he considered the Executive magistracy as nothing more than an institution for carrying the will of the Legislature into effect, that the person or persons ought to be appointed by and accountable to the Legislature only, which was the depositary of the supreme will of the Society. As they were the best judges of the business which ought to be done by the Executive department, and consequently of the number necessary from time to time for doing it, he wished the number might not be fixed but that the legislature should be at liberty to appoint one or more as experience might dictate.

**Mr. WILSON** preferred a single magistrate, as giving most energy dispatch and responsibility to the office. He did not consider the Prerogatives of the British Monarch as a proper guide in defining the Executive powers. Some of these prerogatives were of Legislative nature. Among others that of war & peace &c. The only powers he conceived strictly Executive were those of executing the laws, and appointing officers, not appertaining to and appointed by the Legislature.

**Mr. GERRY** favored the policy of annexing a Council to the Executive in order to give weight & inspire confidence. Mr. RANDOLPH strenuously opposed a unity in the Executive magistracy. He regarded it as the foetus of monarchy. We had he said no motive to be governed by the British Governmt. as our prototype. He did not mean however to throw censure on that Excellent fabric. If we were in a situation to copy it he did not know that he should be opposed to it; but the fixt genius of the people of America required a different form of Government. He could not see why the great requisites for the Executive department, vigor, despatch & responsibility could not be found in three men, as well as in one man. The Executive ought to be independent. It ought therefore in order to support its independence to consist of more than one.

**Mr. WILSON** said that unity in the Executive instead of being the fetus of monarchy would be the best safeguard against tyranny. He repeated that he was not governed by the British Model which was inapplicable to the situation of this Country; the extent of which was so great, and the manners so republican, that nothing but a great confederated Republic would do for it. Mr. Wilson's motion for a single magistrate was postponed by common consent, the Committee seeming unprepared for any decision on it; and the first part of the clause agreed to, viz-"that a National Executive be instituted."

Mr. MADISON thought it would be proper, before a choice shd. be made between a unity and a plurality in the Executive, to fix the extent of the Executive authority; that as certain powers were in their nature Executive, and must be given to that depart-mt. whether administered by one or more persons, a definition of their extent would assist the judgment in determining how far they might be safely entrusted to a single officer. He accordingly moved that so much of the clause before the Committee as related to the powers of the Executive shd. be struck out & that after the words "that a national Executive ought to be instituted" there be inserted the words following viz. "with power to carry into effect the national laws, to appoint to offices in cases not otherwise provided for, and to execute such other powers "not Legislative nor Judiciary in their nature," as may from time to time be delegated by the national Legislature." The words "not legislative nor judiciary in their nature" were added to the proposed amendment in consequence of a suggestion by Genl. Pinkney that improper powers might otherwise be delegated.

Mr. WILSON seconded this motion-

Mr. PINKNEY moved to amend the amendment by striking out the last member of it; viz: "and to execute such other powers not Legislative nor Judiciary in their nature as may from time to time be delegated." He said they were unnecessary, the object of them being included in the "power to carry into effect the national laws."

Mr. RANDOLPH seconded the motion.

Mr. MADISON did not know that the words were absolutely necessary, or even the preceding words-"to appoint to offices &c. the whole being perhaps included in the first member of the proposition. He did not however see any inconveniency in retaining them, and cases might happen in which they might serve to prevent doubts and misconstructions.

In consequence of the motion of Mr. Pinkney, the question on Mr. Madison's motion was divided; and the words objected to by Mr. Pinkney struck out; by the votes of Connecticut, N. Y. N. J. Pena. Del. N. C. & Geo. agst. Mass. Virga. & S. Carolina the preceding part of the motion being first agreed to; Connecticut divided, all the other States in the affirmative. The next clause in Resolution 7, relating to the mode of appointing, & the duration of, the Executive being under consideration,

**Mr. WILSON** said he was almost unwilling to declare the mode which he wished to take place, being apprehensive that it might appear chimerical. He would say however at least that in theory he was for an election by the people. Experience, particularly in N. York & Massts., shewed that an election of the first magistrate by the people at large, was both a convenient & successful mode. The objects of choice in such cases must be persons whose merits have general notoriety.

**Mr. SHERMAN** was for the appointment by the Legislature, and for making him absolutely dependent on that body, as it was the will of that which was to be executed. An independence of the Executive on the supreme Legislature, was in his opinion the very essence of tyranny if there was any such thing.

**Mr. WILSON** moves that the blank for the term of duration should be filled with three years, observing at the same time that he preferred this short period, on the supposition that a reeligibility would be provided for.

**Mr. PINKNEY** moves for seven years.

**Mr. SHERMAN** was for three years, and agst. the doctrine of rotation as throwing out of office the men best qualified to execute its duties.

**Mr. MASON** was for seven years at least, and for prohibiting a re-eligibility as the best expedient both for preventing the effect of a false complaisance on the side of the Legislature towards unfit characters; and a temptation on the side of the Executive to intrigue with the Legislature for a re-appointment.

**Mr. BEDFORD** was strongly opposed to so long a term as seven years. He begged the committee to consider what the situation of the Country would be, in case the first magistrate should be saddled on it for such a period and it should be found on trial that he did not possess the qualifications ascribed to him, or should lose them after his appointment. An impeachment he said would be no cure for this evil, as an impeachment would reach misfeasance only, not incapacity. He was for a triennial election, and for an ineligibility after a period of nine years.

On the question for seven years, Massts. dividd. Cont. no. N.

Y. ay. N. J. ay. Pena. ay. Del. ay. Virga. ay. N. C. no. S. C. no. Geor. no. There being 5 ays, 4 noes, 1 divd., a question was asked whether a majority had voted in the affirmative? The President decided that it was an affirmative vote.

The mode of appointing the Executive was the next question.

**Mr. WILSON** renewed his declarations in favor of an appointment by the people. He wished to derive not only both branches of the Legislature from the people, without the intervention of the State Legislatures but the Executive also; in order to make them as independent as possible of each other, as well as of the States;

**Col. MASON** favors the idea, but thinks it impracticable. He wishes however that Mr. Wilson might have time to digest it into his own form.-the clause "to be chosen by the National Legislature"-was accordingly postponed.-

**Mr. RUTLIDGE** suggests an election of the Executive by the second branch only of the national Legislature.

The Committee then rose and the House

Adjourned.

## Thursday July 19, 1787
## IN CONVENTION

On reconsideration of the vote rendering the Executive re-eligible a 2d. time, Mr. MARTIN moved to reinstate the words, "to be ineligible a 2d. time."

**Mr. GOVERNEUR MORRIS**. It is necessary to take into one view all that relates to the establishment of the Executive; on the due formation of which must depend the efficacy & utility of the Union among the present and future States. It has been a maxim in Political Science that Republican Government is not adapted to a large extent of Country, because the energy of the Executive Magistracy can not reach the extreme parts of it. Our Country is an extensive one. We must either then renounce the blessings of the Union, or provide an Executive with sufficient vigor to pervade every part of it. This subject was of so much importance that he hoped to be indulged in an extensive view of it. One great object of the Executive is to controul the Legislature. The Legislature will continually seek to aggrandize & perpetuate themselves; and will seize those critical moments produced by war, invasion or convulsion for that purpose. It is necessary then that the Executive Magistrate should be the guardian of the people, even of the lower classes, agst. Legislative tyranny, against the Great & the wealthy who in the course of things will necessarily compose the Legislative body. Wealth tends to corrupt the mind & to nourish its love of power, and to stimulate it to oppression. History proves this to be the spirit of the opulent. The check provided in the 2d. branch was not meant as a check on Legislative usurpations of power, but on the abuse of lawful powers, on the propensity in the 1st. branch to legislate too much to run into projects of paper money & similar expedients. It is no check on Legislative tyranny. On the contrary it may favor it, and if the 1st. branch can be seduced may find the means of success. The Executive therefore ought to be so constituted as to be the great protector of the Mass of the people. -It is the duty of the Executive to appoint the officers & to command the forces of the Republic: to appoint 1. ministerial officers for the administration of public affairs. 2. officers for the dispensation of Justice. Who will be the best Judges whether these appointments be well made? The people at large, who will know, will see, will feel the effects of them. Again who can judge so well of the discharge of military duties for the protection & security of the people, as the people themselves who are to be protected & secured? -He finds too that the Executive is not to be re-eligible. What effect will this have?

1. it will destroy the great incitement to merit public esteem by taking away the hope of being rewarded with a reappointment. It may give a dangerous turn to one of the strongest passions in the human breast. The love of fame is the great spring to noble & illustrious actions. Shut the Civil road to Glory & he may be compelled to seek it by the sword.

2. It will tempt him to make the most of the short space of time allotted him, to accumulate wealth and provide for his friends.

3. It will produce violations of the very constitution it is meant to secure. In moments of pressing danger the tried abilities and established character of a favorite Magistrate will prevail over respect for the forms of the Constitution. The Executive is also to be impeachable. This is a dangerous part of the plan. It will hold him in such dependence that he will be no check on the Legislature, will not be a firm guardian of the people and of the public interest. He will be the tool of a faction, of some leading demagogue in the Legislature. These then are the faults of the Executive establishment as now proposed. Can no better establishmt. be devised? If he is to be the Guardian of the people let him be appointed by the people? If he is to be a check on the Legislature let him not be impeachable. Let him be of short duration, that he may with propriety be re-eligible. It has been said that the candidates for this office will not be known to the people. If they be known to the Legislature, they must have such a notoriety and eminence of Character, that they can not possibly be unknown to the people at large. It cannot be possible that a man shall have sufficiently distinguished himself to merit this high trust without having his character proclaimed by fame throughout the Empire. As to the danger from an unimpeachable magistrate he could not regard it as formidable. There must be certain great officers of State; a minister of finance, of war, of foreign affairs &c. These he presumes will exercise their functions in subordination to the Executive, and will be amenable by impeachment to the public Justice. Without these ministers the Executive can do nothing of consequence. He

suggested a biennial election of the Executive at the time of electing the 1st. branch, and the Executive to hold over, so as to prevent any interregnum in the administration. An election by the people at large throughout so great an extent of country could not be influenced, by those little combinations and those momentary lies which often decide popular elections within a narrow sphere. It will probably, be objected that the election will be influenced by the members of the Legislature; particularly of the 1st. branch, and that it will be nearly the same thing with an election by the Legislature itself. It could not be denied that such an influence would exist. But it might be answered that as the Legislature or the candidates for it would be divided, the enmity of one part would counteract the friendship of another: that if the administration of the Executive were good, it would be unpopular to oppose his re-election, if bad it ought to be opposed & a reappointmt. prevented; and lastly that in every view this indirect dependence on the favor of the Legislature could not be so mischievous as a direct dependence for his appointment. He saw no alternative for making the Executive independent of the Legislature but either to give him his office for life, or make him eligible by the people-Again, it might be objected that two years would be too short a duration. But he believes that as long as he should behave himself well, he would be continued in his place. The extent of the Country would secure his re-election agst. the factions & discontents of particular States. It deserved consideration also that such an ingredient in the plan would render it extremely palatable to the people. These were the general ideas which occurred to him on the subject, and which led him to wish & move that the whole constitution of the Executive might undergo reconsideration.

**Mr. RANDOLPH** urged the motion of Mr. L. Martin for restoring the words making the Executive ineligible a 2d. time. If he ought to be independent, he should not be left under a temptation to court a re-appointment. If he should be re- appointable by the Legislature, he will be no check on it. His revisionary power will be of no avail. He had always thought & contended as he still did that the danger apprehended by the little States was chimerical; but those who thought otherwise ought to be peculiarly anxious for the motion. If the Executive be appointed, as has been determined, by the Legislature, he will probably be appointed either by joint ballot of both houses, or be nominated by the 1st. and appointed by the 2d. branch. In either case the large States will preponderate. If he is to court the same influence for his re-appointment, will he not make his revisionary power, and all the other functions of his administration subservient to the views of the large States. Besides, is there not great reason to apprehend that in case he should be re-eligible, a false complaisance in the Legislature might lead them to continue an unfit man in office in preference to a fit one. It has been said that a constitutional bar to reappointment will inspire unconstitutional endeavours to perpetuate himself. It may be answered that his endeavours can have no effect unless the people be corrupt to such a degree as to render all precautions hopeless: to which may be added that this argument supposes him to be more powerful & dangerous, than other arguments which have been used, admit, and consequently calls for stronger fetters on his authority. He thought an election by the Legislature with an incapacity to be elected a second time would be more acceptable to the people that the plan suggested by Mr. Govr. Morris.

**Mr. KING**. did not like the ineligibility. He thought there was great force in the remark of Mr. Sherman, that he who has proved himself to be most fit for an Office, ought not to be excluded by the constitution from holding it. He would therefore prefer any other reasonable plan that could be substituted. He was much disposed to think that in such cases the people at large would chuse wisely. There was indeed some difficulty arising from the improbability of a general concurrence of the people in favor of any one man. On the whole he was of opinion that an appointment by electors chosen by the people for the purpose, would be liable to fewest objections.

**Mr. PATTERSON**'s ideas nearly coincided he said with those of Mr. King. He proposed that the Executive should be appointed by Electors to be chosen by the States in a ratio that would allow one elector to the smallest and three to the largest States. Mr. WILSON. It seems to be the unanimous sense that the Executive should not be appointed by the Legislature, unless he be rendered in-eligible a 2d. time: he perceived with pleasure that the idea was gaining ground, of an election mediately or immediately by the people.

**Mr. MADISON**. If it be a fundamental principle of free

Govt. that the Legislative, Executive & Judiciary powers should be separately exercised, it is equally so that they be independently exercised. There is the same & perhaps greater reason why the Executive shd. be independent of the Legislature, than why the Judiciary should: A coalition of the two former powers would be more immediately & certainly dangerous to public liberty. It is essential then that the appointment of the Executive should either be drawn from some source, or held by some tenure, that will give him a free agency with regard to the Legislature. This could not be if he was to be appointable from time to time by the Legislature. It was not clear that an appointment in the 1st. instance even with an eligibility afterwards would not establish an improper connection between the two departments. Certain it was that the appointment would be attended with intrigues and contentions that ought not to be unnecessarily admitted. He was disposed for these reasons to refer the appointment to some other source. The people at large was in his opinion the fittest in itself. It would be as likely as any that could be devised to produce an Executive Magistrate of distinguished Character. The people generally could only know & vote for some Citizen whose merits had rendered him an object of general attention & esteem. There was one difficulty however of a serious nature attending an immediate choice by the people. The right of suffrage was much more diffusive in the Northern than the Southern States; and the latter could have no influence in the election on the score of the Negroes. The substitution of electors obviated this difficulty and seemed on the whole to be liable to fewest objections.

**Mr. GERRY**. If the Executive is to be elected by the Legislature he certainly ought not to be re-eligible. This would make him absolutely dependent. He was agst. a popular election. The people are uninformed, and would be misled by a few designing men. He urged the expediency of an appointment of the Executive by Electors to be chosen by the State Executives. The people of the States will then choose the 1st. branch: The legislatures of the States the 2d. branch of the National Legislature, and the Executives of the States, the National Executive. This he thought would form a strong attachnt. in the States to the National System. The popular mode of electing the chief Magistrate would certainly be the worst of all. If he should be so elected & should do his duty, he will be turned out for it like Govr. Bowdoin in Massts. & President Sullivan in N. Hamshire.

On the question on Mr. Govr. Morris motion to reconsider generally the constitution of the Executive. Mas. ay. Ct. ay. N. J. ay & all the others ay.

**Mr. ELSEWORTH** moved to strike out the appointmt. by the Natl. Legislature, and insert "to be chosen by electors appointed, by the Legislatures of the States in the following ratio; towit-one for each State not exceeding 200,000 inhabts. two for each above yt. number & not exceeding 300,000. and three for each State exceeding 300,000.

**Mr. BROOME** 2ded. the motion

**Mr. RUTLIDGE** was opposed to all the modes except the appointmt. by the Natl. Legislature. He will be sufficiently independent, if he be not re-eligible.

**Mr. GERRY** preferred the motion of Mr. Elseworth to an appointmt. by the Natl. Legislature, or by the people; tho' not to an appt. by the State Executives. He moved that the electors proposed by Mr. E. should be 25 in number, and allotted in the following proportion. to N. H. 1. to Mas. 3. to R. I. 1. to Cont. 2. to N. Y. 2. N. J. 2. Pa. 3. Del. 1. Md. 2. Va. 3. N. C. 2. S. C. 2. Geo. 1.

The question as moved by Mr. Elseworth being divided, on the 1st. part shall ye. Natl. Executive be appointed by Electors? Mas. divd. Cont. ay. N. J. ay. Pa. ay. Del. ay. Md. ay. Va. ay. N. C. no. S. C. no. Geo. no.

On 2d. part shall the Electors be chosen by State Legislatures? Mas. ay. Cont. ay. N. J. ay. Pa. ay. Del. ay. Md. ay. Va. no. N. C. ay. S. C. no. Geo. ay.

The part relating to the ratio in which the States sd. chuse electors was postponed nem. con.

**Mr. L. MARTIN** moved that the Executive be ineligible a 2d. time.

**Mr. WILLIAMSON** 2ds. the motion. He had no great confidence in the Electors to be chosen for the special purpose. They would not be the most respectable citizens; but persons not occupied in the high offices of Govt. They would be liable to undue influence, which might the more readily be practised as some of them will probably be in appointment 6 or 8 months before the object of it comes on.

**Mr. ELSEWORTH** supposed any persons might be appointed Electors, excepting solely, members of the Natl. Legislature.

On the question shall he be ineligible a 2d. time? Mas. no. Ct. no. N. J. no. Pa. no. Del. no. Md. no. Va. no. N. C. ay. S. C. ay. Geo. no.

On the question Shall the Executive continue for 7 years? It passed in the negative Mas. divd. Cont. ay. N. J. no. Pa. no. Del. no. Md. no. Va. no. N. C. divd. S. C. ay. Geo. ay.

**Mr. KING** was afraid we shd. shorten the term too much.

**Mr. Govr. MORRIS** was for a short term, in order to avoid impeachts. which wd.. be otherwise necessary.

**Mr. BUTLER** was agst. a frequency of the elections. Geo. & S. C. were too distant to send electors often.

**Mr. ELSEWORTH** was for 6. years. If the elections be too frequent, the Executive will not be firm eno'. There must be duties which will make him unpopular for the moment. There will be outs as well as ins. His administration therefore will be attacked and misrepresented.

**Mr. WILLIAMSON** was for 6 years. The expence will be considerable & ought not to be unnecessarily repeated. If the Elections are too frequent, the best men will not undertake the service and those of an inferior character will be liable to be corrupted.

On question for 6 years? Mas. ay. Cont. ay. N. J. ay. Pa ay. Del. no. Md

. ay. Va. ay. N. C. ay. S. C. ay. Geo. ay.

Adjourned

## Tuesday July 24, 1787
## IN CONVENTION

The appointment of the Executive by Electors reconsidered.

**Mr. HOUSTON** moved that he be appointed by the "Natl. Legislature," instead of "Electors appointed by the State Legislatures" according to the last decision of the mode. He dwelt chiefly on the improbability, that capable men would undertake the service of Electors from the more distant States.

**Mr. SPAIGHT** seconded the motion.

**Mr. GERRY** opposed it. He thought there was no ground to apprehend the danger urged by Mr. Houston. The election of the Executive Magistrate will be considered as of vast importance and will excite great earnestness. The best men, the Governours of the States will not hold it derogatory from their character to be the electors. If the motion should be agreed to, it will be necessary to make the Executive ineligible a 2d. time, in order to render him independent of the Legislature; which was an idea extremely repugnant to his way of thinking.

**Mr. STRONG** supposed that there would be no necessity, if the Executive should be appointed by the Legislature, to make him ineligible a 2d. time; as new elections of the Legislature will have intervened; and he will not depend for his 2d. appointment on the same sett of men as his first was recd. from. It had been suggested that gratitude for his past appointment wd. produce the same effect as dependence for his future appointment. He thought very differently. Besides this objection would lie agst. the Electors who would be objects of gratitude as well as the Legislature. It was of great importance not to make the Govt. too complex which would be the case if a new sett of men like the Electors should be introduced into it. He thought also that the first characters in the States would not feel sufficient motives to undertake the office of Electors.

**Mr. WILLIAMSON** was for going back to the original ground; to elect the Executive for 7 years and render him ineligible a 2d. time. The proposed Electors would certainly not be men of the 1st. nor even of the 2d. grade in the States. These would all prefer a seat either in the Senate or the other branch of the Legislature. He did not like the Unity in the Executive. He had wished the Executive power to be lodged in three men taken from three districts into which the States should be divided. As the Executive is to have a kind of veto on the laws, and there is an essential difference of interests between the N. & S. States, particularly in the carrying trade, the power will be dangerous, if the Executive is to be taken from part of the Union, to the part from which he is not taken. The case is different here from what it is in England; where there is a sameness of interests throughout the Kingdom. Another objection agst. a single Magistrate is that he will be an elective King, and will feel the spirit of one. He will spare no pains to keep himself in for life, and will then lay a train for the succession of his children. It was pretty certain he thought that we should at some time or other have a King; but he wished no precaution to be omitted that might postpone the event as long as possible. -Ineligibility a 2d. time appeared to him to be the best precaution. With this precaution he had no objection to a longer term than 7 years. He would go as far as 10 or 12 years.

Mr. GERRY moved that the Legislatures of the States should vote by ballot for the Executive in the same proportions as it had been proposed they should chuse electors; and that in case a majority of the votes should not center on the same person, the 1st. branch of the Natl. Legislature should chuse two out of the 4 candidates having most votes, and out of these two, the 2d. branch should chuse the Executive.

Mr. KING seconded the motion-and on the Question to postpone in order to take it into consideration. The noes were so predominant, that the States were not counted.

Question on Mr. Houston's motion that the Executive be appd. by Nal. Legislature

N. H. ay. Mas. ay. Ct. no. N. J. ay. Pa. no. Del. ay. Md. no. Va. no. N. C. ay. S. C. ay. Geo. ay.

Mr. L. MARTIN & Mr. GERRY moved to re-instate the ineligibility of the Executive a 2d. time.

Mr. ELSEWORTH. With many this appears a natural consequence of his being elected by the Legislature. It was not the case with him. The Executive he thought should be reelected if his conduct proved him worthy of it. And he will be more likely to render himself, worthy of it if he be rewardable with it. The most eminent characters also will be more willing to accept the trust under this condition, than if they foresee a necessary degradation at a fixt period.

**Mr. GERRY**. That the Executive shd. be independent of the Legislature is a clear point. The longer the duration of his appointment the more will his dependence be diminished. It will be better then for him to continue 10, 15, or even 20, years and be ineligible afterwards.

**Mr. KING** was for making him re-eligible. This is too great an advantage to be given up for the small effect it will have on his dependence, if impeachments are to lie. He considered these as rendering the tenure during pleasure.

**Mr. L. MARTIN**, suspending his motion as to the ineligibility, moved "that the appointmt. of the Executive shall continue for Eleven years.

**Mr. GERRY** suggested fifteen years

**Mr. KING** twenty years. This is the medium life of princes.

**Mr. DAVIE** Eight years

**Mr. WILSON**. The difficulties & perplexities into which the House is thrown proceed from the election by the Legislature which he was sorry had been reinstated. The inconveniency of this mode was such that he would agree to almost any length of time in order to get rid of the dependence which must result from it. He was persuaded that the longest term would not be equivalent to a proper mode of election; unless indeed it should be during good behaviour. It seemed to be supposed that at a certain advance in life, a continuance in office would cease to be agreeable to the officer, as well as desirable to the public. Experience had shewn in a variety of instances that both a capacity & inclination for public service existed-in very advanced stages. He mentioned the instance of a Doge of Venice who was elected after he was 80 years of age. The popes have generally been elected at very advanced periods, and yet in no case had a more steady or a better concerted policy been pursued than in the Court of Rome. If the Executive should come into office at 35. years of age, which he presumes may happen & his continuance should be fixt at 15 years. at the age of 50. in the very prime of life, and with all the aid of experience, he must be cast aside like a useless hulk. What an irreparable loss would the British Jurisprudence have sustained, had the age of 50. been fixt there as the ultimate limit of capacity or readiness to serve the public. The great luminary [Ld. Mansfield] held his seat for thirty years after his arrival at that age. Notwithstanding what had been done he could not but hope that a better mode of election would yet be adopted; and one that would be more agreeable to the general sense of the House. That time might be given for further deliberation he wd. move that the present question be postponed till tomorrow.

**Mr. BROOM** seconded the motion to postpone.

**Mr. GERRY**. We seem to be entirely at a loss on this head. He would suggest whether it would not be adviseable to refer the clause relating to the Executive to the Committee of detail to be appointed. Perhaps they will be able to hit on something that may unite the various opinions which have been thrown out.

**Mr. WILSON**. As the great difficulty seems to spring from the mode of election, he wd. suggest a mode which had not been mentioned. It was that the Executive be elected for 6 years by a small number, not more than 15 of the Natl. Legislature, to be drawn from it, not by ballot, but by lot and who should retire immediately and make the election without separating. By this mode intrigue would be avoided in the first instance, and the dependence would be diminished. This was not he said a digested idea and might be liable to strong objections.

**Mr. Govr. MORRIS**. Of all possible modes of appointment that by the Legislature is the worst. If the Legislature is to appoint, and to impeach or to influence the impeachment, the Executive will be the mere creature of it. He had been opposed to the impeachment but was now convinced that impeachments must be provided for, if the appt. was to be of any duration. No man wd. say, that an Executive known to be in the pay of an Enemy, should not be removeable in some way or other. He had been charged heretofore [by Col. Mason] with inconsistency in pleading for confidence in the Legislature on some occasions, & urging a distrust on others. The charge was not well founded. The Legislature is worthy of unbounded confidence in some respects, and liable to equal distrust in others. When their interest coincides precisely with that of their Constituents, as happens in many of their Acts, no abuse of trust is to be apprehended. When a strong personal interest happens to be opposed to the general interest, the Legislature can not be too much distrusted. In all public bodies there are two parties. The

Executive will necessarily be more connected with one than with the other. There will be a personal interest therefore in one of the parties to oppose as well as in the other to support him. Much had been said of the intrigues that will be practised by the Executive to get into office. Nothing had been said on the other side of the intrigues to get him out of office. Some leader of party will always covet his seat, will perplex his administration, will cabal with the Legislature, till he succeeds in supplanting him. This was the way in which the King of England was got out, he meant the real King, the Minister. This was the way in which Pitt [Ld. Chatham] forced himself into place. Fox was for pushing the matter still farther. If he carried his India bill, which he was very near doing, he would have made the Minister, the King in form almost as well as in sub-stance. Our President will be the British Minister, yet we are about to make him appointable by the Legislature. Something had been said of the danger of Monarchy. If a good government should not now be formed, if a good organization of the Execuve should not be provided, he doubted whether we should not have something worse than a limited Monarchy. In order to get rid of the depen-dence of the Executive on the Legislature, the expedient of making him ineligible a 2d. time had been devised. This was as much as to say we shd. give him the benefit of experience, and then deprive ourselves of the use of it. But make him ineligible a 2d. time-and prolong his duration even to 15- years, will he by any wonderful interposition of providence at that period cease to be a man? No he will be unwilling to quit his exaltation, the road to his object thro' the Constitution will be shut; he will be in possession of the sword, a civil war will ensue, and the Commander of the victorious army on which ever side, will be the despot of America. This consider-ation renders him particularly anxious that the Executive should be properly constituted. The vice here would not, as in some other parts of the system be curable. It is the most difficult of all rightly to balance the Executive. Make him too weak: The Legislature will usurp his powers: Make him too strong. He will usurp on the Leg-islature. He preferred a short period, a re-eligibility, but a different mode of election. A long period would prevent an adoption of the plan: it ought to do so. He shd. himself be afraid to trust it. He was not prepared to decide on Mr. Wilson's mode of election just hinted by him. He thought it deserved consideration It would be better that chance sd. decide than intrigue.

On a question to postpone the consideration of the Resolution on the subject of the Executive

N. H. no. Mas. no. Ct. ay. N. J. no. Pa. ay. Del. divd. Md. ay. Va. ay. N. C. no. S. C. no. Geo. no.

**Mr. WILSON** then moved that the Executive be chosen every ------- years by ------- Electors to be taken by lot from the Natl Legislature who shall proceed immediately to the choice of the Executive and not separate until it be made."

**Mr. CARROL** 2ds. the motion

**Mr. GERRY**. this is committing too much to chance. If the lot should fall on a sett of unworthy men, an unworthy Executive must be saddled on the Country. He thought it had been demonstrated that no possible mode of electing by the Legislature could be a good one.

**Mr. KING**. The lot might fall on a majority from the same State which wd. ensure the election of a man from that State. We ought to be governed by reason, not by chance. As nobody seemed to be satisfied, he wished the matter to be postponed

**Mr. WILSON** did not move this as the best mode. His opinion remained unshaken that we ought to resort to the people for the election. He seconded the postponement.

**Mr. Govr. MORRIS** observed that the chances were almost infinite agst. a majority of electors from the same State.

On a question whether the last motion was in order, it was determined in the affirmative; 7. ays. 4 noes.

On the question of postponent. it was agreed to nem. con.

**Mr. CARROL** took occasion to observe that he considered the clause declaring that direct taxation on the States should be in proportion to representation, previous to the obtaining an actual census, as very objectionable, and that he reserved to himself the right of opposing it, if the Report of the Committee of detail should leave it in the plan.

**Mr. Govr. MORRIS** hoped the Committee would strike out the whole of the clause proportioning direct taxation to representation. He had only meant it as a bridge to assist us over a certain gulph; having passed the gulph the bridge may be removed. He thought the principle laid down with so much strictness, liable to strong objections

On a ballot for a Committee to report a Constitution conformable to the Resolutions passed by the Convention, the members chosen were Mr. Rutlidge, Mr. Randolph, Mr. Ghorum, Mr. Elseworth, Mr. Wilson-

On motion to discharge the Come. of the whole from the propositions submitted to the Convention by Mr. C. Pinkney as the basis of a constitution, and to refer them to the Committee of detail just appointed, it was agd. to nem: con.

A like motion was then made & agreed to nem: con: with respect to the propositions of Mr. Patterson

Adjourned.

**Tuesday July 25, 1787**
**IN CONVENTION**

Clause relating to the Executive again under consideration.

**Mr. ELSEWORTH** moved "that the Executive be appointed by the Legislature," except when the magistrate last chosen shall have continued in office the whole term for which he was chosen, & be reeligible, in which case the choice shall be by Electors appointed by the Legislatures of the States for that purpose." By this means a deserving magistrate may be reelected without making him dependent on the Legislature.

**Mr. GERRY** repeated his remark that an election at all by the Natl. Legislature was radically and incurably wrong; and moved that the Executive be appointed by the Governours & Presidents of the States, with advice of their Councils, and where there are no Councils by Electors chosen by the Legislatures. The executives to vote in the following proportions: viz-

**Mr. MADISON**. There are objections agst. every mode that has been, or perhaps can be proposed. The election must be made either by some existing authority under the Natil. or State Constitutions-or by some special authority derived from the people-or by the people themselves. -The two Existing authorities under the Natl. Constitution wd. be the Legislative & Judiciary. The latter he presumed was out of the question. The former was in his Judgment liable to insuperable objections. Besides the general influence of that mode on the independence of the Executive, 1. the election of the Chief Magistrate would agitate & divide the legislature so much that the public interest would materially suffer by it. Public bodies are always apt to be thrown into contentions, but into more violent ones by such occasions than by any others. 2. the candidate would intrigue with the Legislature, would derive his appointment from the predominant faction, and be apt to render his administration subservient to its views. 3. The Ministers of foreign powers would have and make use of, the opportunity to mix their intrigues & influence with the Election. Limited as the powers of the Executive are, it will be an object of great moment with the great rival powers of Europe who have American possessions, to have at the head of our Governmt. a man attached to their respective politics & interests. No pains, nor perhaps expense, will be spared, to gain from the Legislature an appointmt. favorable to their wishes. Germany & Poland are witnesses of this danger. In the former, the election of the Head of the Empire, till it became in a manner hereditary, interested all Europe, and was much influenced by foreign interference. In the latter, altho' the elective Magistrate has very little real power, his election has at all times produced the most eager interference of forign princes, and has in fact at length slid entirely into foreign hands. The existing authorities in the States are the Legislative, Executive & Judiciary. The appointment of the Natl. Executive by the first, was objectionable in many points of view, some of which had been already mentioned. He would mention one which of itself would decide his opinion. The Legislatures of the States had betrayed a strong propensity to a variety of pernicious measures. One object of the Natl. Legislre. was to controul this propensity. One object of the Natl. Executive, so far as it would have a negative on the laws, was to controul the Natl. Legislature, so far as it might be infected with a similar propensity. Refer the appointmt. of the Natl. Executive to the State Legislatures, and this controuling purpose may be defeated. The Legislatures can & will act with some kind of regular plan, and will promote the appointmt. of a man who will not oppose himself to a favorite object. Should a majority of the Legislatures at the time of election have the same object, or different objects of the same kind, The Natl. Executive would be rendered subservient to them. -An appointment by the State Executives, was liable among other objections to this insuperable one, that being standing bodies, they could & would be courted, and intrigued with by the Candidates, by their partizans, and by the Ministers of foreign powers. The State Judiciarys had not & he presumed wd. not be proposed as a proper source of appointment. The option before us then lay between an appointment by Electors chosen by the people-and an immediate appointment by the people. He thought the former mode free from many of the objections which had been urged agst. it, and greatly preferable to an appointment by the Natl. Legislature. As the electors would be chosen for the occasion, would meet at once, & proceed immediately to an appointment, there would be very little opportunity for cabal, or corruption. As a farther precaution, it might be required that they should meet at some place, distinct from the seat of Govt. and even that no person within a certain distance of the place at the time shd. be eligible. This Mode however had been rejected so recently & by so great a majority that it probably would not be proposed anew. The remaining mode was an election by the people or rather by the qualified part of them, at large: With all its imperfections he liked this best. He would not repeat either the general argumts. for or the objections agst. this mode. He would only take notice of two difficulties which he admitted to have weight. The first arose from the disposition in the people to prefer a Citizen of their own State, and the disadvantage this wd. throw on the smaller States. Great as this objection might be he did not think it equal to such as lay agst. every other mode which had been proposed. He thought too that some expedient might be hit upon that would obviate it. The second difficulty arose from the disproportion of qualified voters in the N. & S. States, and the disadvantages which this mode would throw on the latter. The answer to this objection was 1. that this disproportion would be continually decreasing under the influence of the Republican laws introduced in the S. States, and the more rapid increase of their population. 2. That local considerations must give way to the general interest. As an individual from the S. States he was willing to make the sacrifice.

**Mr. ELSEWORTH**. The objection drawn from the different sizes of the States, is unanswerable. The Citizens of the largest States would invariably prefer the Candidate within the State; and the largest States wd. invariably have the man.

Question on Mr. Elseworth's motion as above.

N. H. ay. Mas. no. Ct ay. N. J. no. Pa. ay. Del. no. Md. ay. Va. no. N. C. no. S. C. no. Geo. no.

**Mr. PINKNEY** moved that the election by the Legislature be qualified with a proviso that no person be eligible for more than 6 years in any twelve years. He thought this would have all the advantage & at the same time avoid in some degree the inconveniency, of an absolute ineligibility a 2d. time.

**Col. MASON** approved the idea. It had the sanction of experience in the instance of Congs. and some of the Executives of the States. It rendered the Executive as effectually independent, as an ineligibility after his first election, and opened the way at the same time for the advantage of his future services. He preferred on the whole the election by the Nati. Legislature: Tho' Candor obliged him to admit, that there was great danger of foreign influence, as had been suggested. This was the most serious objection with him that had been urged.

Mr. BUTLER. The two great evils to be avoided are cabal at home, & influence from abroad. It will be difficult to avoid either if the Election be made by the Natl. Legislature. On the other hand: The Govt. should not be made so complex & unwieldy as to disgust the States. This would be the case, if the election shd. be referred to the people. He liked best an election by Electors chosen by the Legislatures of the States. He was agst. are-eligibility at all events. He was also agst. a ratio of votes in the States. An equality should prevail in this case. The reasons for departing from it do not hold in the case of the Executive as in that of the Legislature.

Mr. GERRY approved of Mr. Pinkney's motion as lessening the evil.

Mr. Govr. MORRIS was agst. a rotation in every case. It formed a political School, in wch we were always governed by the scholars, and not by the Masters. The evils to be guarded agst. in this case are 1. the undue influence of the Legislature. 2. instability of Councils. 3. misconduct in office. To guard agst. the first, we run into the second evil. We adopt a rotation which produces instability of Councils. To avoid Sylla we fall into Charibdis. A change of men is ever followed by a change of measures. We see this fully exemplified in the vicissitudes among ourselves, particularly in the State of Pena. The self-sufficiency of a victorious party scorns to tread in the paths of their predecessors. Rehoboam will not imitate Soloman. 2. the Rotation in office will not prevent intrigue and dependence on the Legislature. The man in office will look forward to the period at which he will become re-eligible. The distance of the period, the improbability of such a protraction of his life will be no obstacle. Such is the nature of man, formed by his benevolent author no doubt for wise ends, that altho' he knows his existence to be limited to a span, he takes his measures as if he were to live for ever. But taking another supposition, the inefficacy of the expedient will be manifest. If the magistrate does not look forward to his re-election to the Executive, he will be pretty sure to keep in view the opportunity of his going into the Legislature itself. He will have little objection then to an extension of power on a theatre where he expects to act a distinguished part; and will be very unwilling to take any step that may endanger his popularity with the Legislature, on his influence over which the figure he is to make will depend. 3. To avoid the third evil, impeachments will be essential, and hence an additional reason agst. an election by the Legislature. He considered an election by the people as the best, by the Legislature as the worst, mode. Putting both these aside, he could not but favor the idea of Mr. Wilson, of introducing a mixture of lot. It will diminish, if not destroy both cabal & dependence.

**Mr. WILLIAMSON** was sensible that strong objections lay agst. an election of the Executive by the Legislature, and that it opened a door for foreign influence. The principal objection agst. an election by the people seemed to be, the disadvantage under which it would place the smaller States. He suggested as a cure for this difficulty, that each man should vote for 3 candidates, One of these he observed would be probably of his own State, the other 2. of some other States; and as probably of a small as a large one.

**Mr. Govr. MORRIS** liked the idea, suggesting as an amendment that each man should vote for two persons one of whom at least should not be of his own State.

**Mr. MADISON** also thought something valuable might be made of the suggestion with the proposed amendment of it. The second best man in this case would probably be the first, in fact. The only objection which occurred was that each Citizen after havg. given his vote for his favorite fellow Citizen, wd. throw away his second on some obscure Citizen of another State, in order to ensure the object of his first choice. But it could hardly be supposed that the Citizens of many States would be so sanguine of having their favorite elected, as not to give their second vote with sincerity to the next object of their choice. It might moreover be provided in favor of the smaller States that the Executive should not be eligible more than times in years from the same State.

**Mr. GERRY**. A popular election in this case is radically vicious. The ignorance of the people would put it in the power of some one set of men dispersed through the Union & acting in Concert to delude them into any appointment. He observed that such a Society of men existed in the Order of the Cincinnati. They are respectable, United, and influencial. They will in fact elect the chief Magistrate in every instance, if the election be referred to the people. His respect for the characters composing this Society could not blind him to the danger & impropriety of throwing such a power into their hands.

**Mr. DICKENSON.** As far as he could judge from the discussions which had taken place during his attendance, insuperable objections lay agst. an election of the Executive by the Natl. Legislature; as also by the Legislatures or Executives of the States. He had long leaned towards an election by the people which he regarded as the best & purest source. Objections he was aware lay agst. this mode, but not so great he thought as agst. the other modes. The greatest difficulty in the opinion of the House seemed to arise from the partiality of the States to their respective Citizens. But, might not this very partiality be turned to a useful purpose. Let the people of each State chuse its best Citizen. The people will know the most eminent characters of their own States, and the people of different States will feel an emulation in selecting those of which they will have the greatest reason to be proud. Out of the thirteen names thus selected, an Executive Magistrate may be chosen either by the Natl. Legislature, or by Electors appointed by it.

On a Question which was moved for postponing Mr. Pinkney's motion; in order to make way for some such proposition as had been hinted by Mr. Williamson & others: it passed in the negative.

N. H. no. Mas. no. Ct. ay. N. J. ay. Pa. ay. Del. no. Md. ay. Va. ay. N. C. no. S. C. no. Geo. no.

On Mr. Pinkney's motion that no person shall serve in the Executive more than 6 years in 12. years, it passed in the negative.

N. H. ay. Mas. ay. Ct. no. N. J. no. Pa. no. Del. no. Md. no. Va. no. N. C. ay. S. C. ay. Geo. ay.

On a motion that the members of the Committee be furnished with copies of the proceedings it was so determined; S. Carolina alone being in the negative.

It was then moved that the members of the House might take copies of the Resolions which had been agreed to; which passed in the negative. N. H. no. Mas. no. Con: ay. N. J. ay. Pa. no. Del. ay. Maryd. no. Va. ay. N. C. ay. S. C. no. Geo. no.

**Mr. GERRY & Mr. BUTLER** moved to refer the resolution relating to the Executive (except the clause making it consist of a single person) to the Committee of detail

**Mr. WILSON** hoped that so important a branch of the System wd. not be committed untill a general principle shd. be fixed by a vote of the House.

**Mr. LANGDON,** was for the Commitment-Adjd.

# Document 2

# U.S. Constitution: Article II

**Section 1- President: his term of office. Electors of President; number and how appointed. Electors to vote on same day. Qualification of President. On whom his duties devolve in case of his removal, death, etc. President's compensation. His oath of office.**

1. The Executive power shall be vested in a President of the United States of America. He shall hold office during the term of four years, and together with the Vice President, chosen for the same term, be elected as follows:

2. Each State shall appoint, in such manner as the Legislature may direct, a number of electors, equal to the whole number of Senators and Representatives to which the State may be entitled in the Congress: but no Senator or Representative, or person holding an office of trust or profit under the United States, shall be appointed an elector. *The electors shall meet in their respective States, and vote by ballot for two persons, of whom one at least shall not be an inhabitant of the same State with themselves. And they shall make a list of all the persons voted for each; which list they shall sign and certify, and transmit sealed to the seat of Government of the United States, directed to the President of the Senate. The President of the Senate shall, in the presence of the Senate and House of Representatives, open all the certificates, and the votes shall then be counted. The person having the greatest number of votes shall be the President, if such number be a majority of the whole number of electors appointed; and if there be more than one who have such majority, and have an equal number of votes, then the House of Representatives shall immediately choose by ballot one of them for President; and if no person have a majority, then from the five highest on the list the said House shall in like manner choose the President. But in choosing the President, the votes shall be taken by States, the representation from*

*each State having one vote; a quorum for this purpose shall consist of a member or members from two-thirds of the States, and a majority of all the States shall be necessary to a choice. In every case, after the choice of the President, the person having the greatest number of votes of the electors shall be the Vice President. But if there should remain two or more who have equal votes, the Senate shall choose from them by ballot the Vice President.* (The clause in italics was superseded by Ammendment XII)

3. The Congress may determine the time of choosing the electors, and the day on which they shall give their votes; which day shall be the same throughout the United States.

4. No person except a natural born Citizen, or a Citizen of the United States, at the time of the adoption of this Constitution, shall be eligible to the office of President; neither shall any person be eligible to that office who shall not have attained to the age of thirty-five years, and been fourteen years a resident within the United States.

5. In case of the removal of the President from office, or of his death, resignation, or inability to discharge the powers and duties of the said office, the same shall devolve on the Vice President, and the Congress may by law provide for the case of removal, death, resignation, or inability, both of the President and Vice President, declaring what officer shall then act as President, and such officer shall act accordingly, until the disability be removed, or a President shall be elected. (This clause has been modified by Amendment XX and Amendment XXV)

6. The President shall, at stated times, receive for his services, a compensation, which shall neither be increased nor diminished during the period for which he shall have been elected, and he shall not receive within that period any other emolument from the United States, or any of them.

7. Before he enter on the execution of his office, he shall take the following oath or affirmation:
"I do solemnly swear (or affirm) that I will faithfully execute the

office of the President of the United States, and will to the best of my ability, preserve, protect and defend the Constitution of the United States."

**Section 2 - President to be Commander-in-Chief. He may require opinions of cabinet officers, etc., may pardon. Treaty-making power. Nomination of certain officers. When President may fill vacancies.**

1. The President shall be Commander-in-Chief of the Army and Navy of the United States, and of the militia of the several States, when called into the actual service of the United States; he may require the opinion, in writing, of the principal officer in each of the executive departments, upon any subject relating to the duties of their respective offices, and he shall have power to grant reprieves and pardons for offenses against the United States, except in cases of impeachment.

2. He shall have power, by and with the advice and consent of the Senate, to make treaties, provided two-thirds of the Senators present concur; and he shall nominate, and by and with the advice and consent of the Senate, shall appoint ambassadors, other public ministers and consuls, judges of the Supreme Court, and all other officers of the United States, whose appointments are not herein otherwise provided for, and which shall be established by law: but the Congress may by law vest the appointment of such inferior officers, as they think proper, in the President alone, in the courts of law, or in the heads of departments.

3. The President shall have the power to fill up all vacancies that may happen during the recess of the Senate, by granting commissions, which shall expire at the end of their next session.

**Section 3 - President shall communicate to Congress. He may convene and adjourn Congress, in case of disagreement, etc. Shall receive ambassadors, execute laws, and commission officers.**

He shall from time to time give to the Congress information of the state of the Union, and recommend to their consideration such measures as he shall judge necessary and expedient; he may, on extraordinary occasions, convene both Houses, or either of them, and in case of disagreement between them, with respect to the time of adjournment, he may adjourn them to such time as he shall think proper; he may receive ambassadors, and other public ministers; he shall take care that the laws be faithfully executed, and shall commission all the officers of the United States.

**Section 4 - All civil offices forfeited for certain crimes.**

The President, Vice President, and all civil officers of the United States, shall be removed from office on impeachment for, and conviction of, treason, bribery, or other high crimes and misdemeanors.

# Document 3

# Federalist Paper No. 68

*The Mode of Electing the President from the* New York Packet. *Friday, March 14, 1788.*

To the People of the State of New York:

THE mode of appointment of the Chief Magistrate of the United States is almost the only part of the system, of any consequence, which has escaped without severe censure, or which has received the slightest mark of approbation from its opponents. The most plausible of these, who has appeared in print, has even deigned to admit that the election of the President is pretty well guarded.1 I venture somewhat further, and hesitate not to affirm, that if the manner of it be not perfect, it is at least excellent. It unites in an eminent degree all the advantages, the union of which was to be wished for.

It was desirable that the sense of the people should operate in the choice of the person to whom so important a trust was to be confided. This end will be answered by committing the right of making it, not to any preestablished body, but to men chosen by the people for the special purpose, and at the particular conjuncture.

It was equally desirable, that the immediate election should be made by men most capable of analyzing the qualities adapted to the station, and acting under circumstances favorable to deliberation, and to a judicious combination of all the reasons and inducements which were proper to govern their choice. A small number of persons, selected by their fellow-citizens from the general mass, will be most likely to possess the information and discernment requisite to such complicated investigations.

It was also peculiarly desirable to afford as little opportunity as possible to tumult and disorder. This evil was not least to be dreaded in the election of a magistrate, who was to have so important an agency in the administration of the government as the President of the United States. But the precautions which have been so happily concerted in the system under consideration, promise an effectual security against this mischief. The choice of SEVERAL, to form an intermediate body of electors, will be much less apt to convulse the community with any extraordinary or violent movements, than the choice of ONE who was himself to be the final object of the public wishes. And as the electors, chosen in each State, are to assemble and vote in the State in which they are chosen, this detached and divided situation will expose them much less to heats and ferments, which might be communicated from them to the people, than if they were all to be convened at one time, in one place.

Nothing was more to be desired than that every practicable obstacle should be opposed to cabal, intrigue, and corruption. These most deadly adversaries of republican government might naturally have been expected to make their approaches from more than one querter, but chiefly from the desire in foreign powers to gain an improper ascendant in our councils. How could they better gratify this, than by raising a creature of their own to the chief magistracy of the Union? But the convention have guarded against all danger of this sort, with the most provident and judicious attention. They have not made the appointment of the President to depend on any preexisting bodies of men, who might be tampered with beforehand to prostitute their votes; but they have referred it in the first instance to an immediate act of the people of America, to be exerted in the choice of persons for the temporary and sole purpose of making the appointment. And they have excluded from eligibility to this trust, all those who from situation might be suspected of too great devotion to the President in office. No senator, representative, or other person holding a place of trust or profit under the United States, can be of the numbers of the electors. Thus without corrupting the body of the people, the immediate agents in the election will at least enter upon the task free from any sinister bias. Their transient existence, and their detached situation, already taken notice of, afford a satisfactory prospect of their continuing so, to the conclusion of it. The business of corruption, when it is to embrace so considerable a number of men, requires time as well as means. Nor would it be found easy suddenly to embark them, dispersed as they would be over thirteen States, in any combinations founded upon motives, which though they could not properly be denominated corrupt, might yet be of a nature to mislead them from their duty.

Another and no less important desideratum was, that the Executive should be independent for his continuance in office on all but the people themselves. He might otherwise be tempted to sacrifice his duty to his complaisance for those whose favor was necessary to the duration of his official consequence. This advantage will also be secured, by making his re-election to depend on a special body of representatives, deputed by the society for the single purpose of making the important choice.

All these advantages will happily combine in the plan devised by the convention; which is, that the people of each State shall choose a number of persons as electors, equal to the number of senators and representatives of such State in the national government, who shall assemble within the State, and vote for some fit person as President. Their votes, thus given, are to be transmitted to the seat of the national government, and the person who may happen to have a majority of the whole number of votes will be the President. But as a majority of the votes might not always happen to centre in one man, and as it might be unsafe to permit less than a majority to be conclusive, it is provided that, in such a contingency, the House of Representatives shall select out of the candidates who shall have the five highest number of votes, the man who in their opinion may be best qualified for the office.

The process of election affords a moral certainty, that the office of President will never fall to the lot of any man who is not in an eminent degree endowed with the requisite qualifications. Talents for low intrigue, and the little arts of popularity, may alone suffice to elevate a man to the first honors in a single State; but it will require other talents, and a different kind of merit, to establish him in the esteem and confidence of the whole Union, or of so considerable a portion of it as would be necessary to make him a successful candidate for the distinguished office of President of the United States. It will not be too strong to say, that there will be a constant probability of seeing the station filled by characters pre-eminent for ability and virtue. And this will be thought no inconsiderable recommendation of the Constitution, by those who are able to estimate the share which the executive in every government must necessarily have in its good or ill administration. Though we cannot acquiesce in the political heresy of the poet who says: "For forms of government let fools contest That which is best administered is best," yet we may safely pronounce, that the true test of a good government is its aptitude and tendency to produce a good administration.

The Vice-President is to be chosen in the same manner with the President; with this difference, that the Senate is to do, in respect to the former, what is to be done by the House of Representatives, in respect to the latter.

The appointment of an extraordinary person, as Vice-President, has been objected to as superfluous, if not mischievous. It has been alleged, that it would have been preferable to have authorized the Senate to elect out of their own body an officer answering that description. But two considerations seem to justify the ideas of the convention in this respect. One is, that to secure at all times the possibility of a definite resolution of the body, it is necessary that the President should have only a casting vote. And to take the senator of any State from his seat as senator, to place him in that of President of the Senate, would be to exchange, in regard to the State from which he came, a constant for a contingent vote. The other consideration is, that as the Vice-President may occasionally become a substitute for the President, in the supreme executive magistracy, all the reasons which recommend the mode of election prescribed for the one, apply with great if not with equal force to the manner of appointing the other. It is remarkable that in this, as in most other instances, the objection which is made would lie against the constitution of this State. We have a Lieutenant-Governor, chosen by the people at large, who presides in the Senate, and is the constitutional substitute for the Governor, in casualties similar to those which would authorize the Vice-President to exercise the authorities and discharge the duties of the President.

PUBIUS.

# Document 4

# Anti-Federalist Paper No. 68

*On the Mode of Electing the President*
*From a speech by William Grayson given to the Virginia ratifying convention*
*on June 18, 1788.*

Mr. [William] GRAYSON. Mr. Chairman, one great objection with me is this: If we advert to..... [the] democratical, aristocratical, or executive branch, we shall find their powers are perpetually varying and fluctuating throughout the whole. Perhaps the democratic branch would be well constructed, were it not for this defect. The executive is still worse, in this respect, than the democratic branch. He is to be elected by a number of electors in the country; but the principle is changed when no person has a majority of the whole number of electors appointed, or when more than one have such a majority, and have an equal number of votes; for then the lower house is to vote by states. It is thus changing throughout the whole. It seems rather founded on accident than any principle of government I ever heard of. We know that there scarcely ever was an election of such an officer without the interposition of foreign powers. Two causes prevail to make them intermeddle in such cases:-one is, to preserve the balance of power; the other, to preserve their trade. These causes have produced interferences of foreign powers in the election of the king of Poland. All the great powers of Europe have interfered in an election which took place not very long ago, and would not let the people choose for themselves. We know how much the powers of Europe have interfered with Sweden. Since the death of Charles XII, that country has been a republican government. Some powers were willing it should be so; some were willing her imbecility should continue; others wished the contrary; and at length the court of France brought about a revolution, which converted it into an absolute government. Can America be free from these interferences? France, after losing

Holland, will wish to make America entirely her own. Great Britain will wish to increase her influence by a still closer connection. It is the interest of Spain, from the contiguity of her possessions in the western hemisphere to the United States, to be in an intimate connection with them, and influence their deliberations, if possible. I think we have every thing, to apprehend from such interferences. It is highly probable the President will be continued in office for life. To gain his favor, they will support him. Consider the means of importance he will have by creating officers. If he has a good understanding with the Senate, they will join to prevent a discovery of his misdeeds. . . .

This quadrennial power cannot be justified by ancient history. There is hardly an instance where a republic trusted its executive so long with much power; nor is it warranted by modern republics. The delegation of power is, in most of them, only for one year.

When you have a strong democratical and a strong aristocratical branch, you may have a strong executive. But when those are weak, the balance will not be preserved, if you give the executive extensive powers for so long a time. As this government is organized, it would be dangerous to trust the President with such powers. How will you punish him if he abuse his power? Will you call him before the Senate? They are his counsellors and partners in crime. Where are your checks? We ought to be extremely cautious in this country. If ever the government be changed, it will probably be into a despotism. The first object in England was to destroy the monarchy; but the aristocratic branch restored him, and of course the government was organized on its ancient principles. But were a revolution to happen here, there would be no means of restoring the government to its former organization. This is a caution to us not to trust extensive powers. I have an extreme objection to the mode of his election. I presume the seven Eastern States will always elect him. As he is vested with the power of making treaties, and as there is a material distinction between the carrying and productive states, the former will be disposed to have him to themselves. He will accommodate himself to their interests in forming treaties, and they will continue him perpetually in office. Thus mutual interest will lead them reciprocally to support one another. It will be a government of a faction, and this observation will apply to every part of it; for, having a majority, they may do what they please. I have made an estimate which shows with what facility they will be able to reelect him. The number of electors is equal to the number of representatives and senators; viz., ninety-one. They are to vote for two persons. They give, therefore, one hundred and eighty-two votes. Let there be forty-five votes for four different candidates, and two for the President. He is one of the five highest, if he have but two votes, which he may easily purchase. In this case, by the 3d clause of the 1st section of the 2d article, the election is to be by the representatives, according to states. Let New Hampshire be for him,-a majority of its . . . . .

| 3 representatives is | 2 | |
|---|---|---|
| Rhode Island | 1 | 1 |
| Connecticut | 5 | 3 |
| New Jersey | 4 | 3 |
| Delaware | 1 | 1 |
| Georgia | 3 | 2 |
| North Carolina | 5 | 3 |

A majority of seven states is 15 Thus the majority of seven states is but 15, while the minority amounts to 50. The total number of voices (91 electors and 65 representatives) is . .

156 Voices in favor of the President are, 2 state electors and 15 representatives ..... 17

139 So that the President may be reelected by the voices of 17 against 139.

It may be said that this is an extravagant case, and will never happen. In my opinion, it will often happen. A person who is a favorite of Congress, if he gets but two votes of electors, may, by the subsequent choice of 15 representatives, be elected President. Surely the possibility of such a case ought to be excluded.

# Document 5

# Anti-Federalist Paper No. 72

*On the Electoral College; On ReEligibility of the President*
*By an anonymous writer "REPUBLICUS," appearing in* THE KENTUCKY
GAZETTE *on March 1, 1788.*

. . I go now to Art. 2, Sec. 1, which vest the supreme continental
executive power in a president-in order to the choice of whom,
the legislative body of each state is empowered to point out to
their constituents some mode of choice, or (to save trouble) may
choose themselves, a certain number of electors, who shall meet
in their respective states, and vote by ballot, for two persons, one
of whom, at least, shall not be an inhabitant of the same state with
themselves. Or in other words, they shall vote for two, one or both
of whom they know nothing of. An extraordinary refinement this,
on the plain simple business of election; and of which the grand
convention have certainly the honor of being the first inventors;
and that for an officer too, of so much importance as a president
- invested with legislative and executive powers; who is to be commander in chief of the army, navy, militia, etc.; grant reprieves and
pardons; have a temporary negative on all bills and resolves; convene and adjourn both houses of congress; be supreme conservator
of laws; commission all officers; make treaties; and who is to continue four years, and is only removable on conviction of treason
or bribery, and triable only by the senate, who are to be his own
council, whose interest in every instance runs parallel with his own,
and who are neither the officers of the people, nor accountable to
them.

Is it then become necessary, that a free people should first
resign their right of suffrage into other hands besides their own,
and then, secondly, that they to whom they resign it should be
compelled to choose men, whose persons, characters, manners, or
principles they know nothing of? And, after all (excepting some

such change as is not likely to happen twice in the same century) to intrust Congress with the final decision at last? Is it necessary, is it rational, that the sacred rights of mankind should thus dwindle down to Electors of electors, and those again electors of other electors? This seems to be degrading them even below the prophetical curse denounced by the good old patriarch, on the offspring of his degenerate son: "servant of servants". . .

Again I would ask (considering how prone mankind are to engross power, and then to abuse it) is it not probable, at least possible, that the president who is to be vested with all this demiomnipotence - who is not chosen by the community; and who consequently, as to them, is irresponsible and independent-that he, I say, by a few artful and dependent emissaries in Congress, may not only perpetuate his own personal administration, but also make it hereditary? By the same means, he may render his suspensive power over the laws as operative and permanent as that of G. the 3d over the acts of the British parliament; and under the modest title of president, may exercise the combined authority of legislation and execution, in a latitude yet unthought of. Upon his being invested with those powers a second or third time, he may acquire such enormous influence-as, added to his uncontrollable power over the army, navy, and militia; together with his private interest in the officers of all these different departments, who are all to be appointed by himself, and so his creatures, in the true political sense of the word; and more especially when added to all this, he has the power of forming treaties and alliances, and calling them to his assistance-that he may, I say, under all these advantages and almost irresistible temptations, on some pretended pique, haughtily and contemptuously, turn our poor lower house (the only shadow of liberty we shall have left) out of doors, and give us law at the bayonet's point. Or, may not the senate, who are nearly in the same situation, with respect to the people, from similar motives and by similar means, erect themselves easily into an oligarchy, towards which they have already attempted so large a stride? To one of which channels, or rather to a confluence of both, we seem to be fast gliding away; and the moment we arrive at it-farewell liberty. . . .

To conclude, I can think of but one source of right to government, or any branch of it-and that is THE PEOPLE. They, and only they, have a right to determine whether they will make laws, or execute them, or do both in a collective body, or by a delegated authority. Delegation is a positive actual investiture. Therefore if any people are subjected to an authority which they have not thus actually chosen-even though they may have tamely submitted to it-yet it is not their legitimate government. They are wholly passive, and as far as they are so, are in a state of slavery. Thank heaven we are not yet arrived at that state. And while we continue to have sense enough to discover and detect, and virtue en(>ugh to detest and oppose every attempt, either of force or fraud, either from without or within, to bring us into it, we never will.

Let us therefore continue united in the cause of rational liberty. Let unity and liberty be our mark as well as our motto. For only such an union can secure our freedom; and division will inevitably destroy it. Thus a mountain of sand may peace meal [sic] be removed by the feeble hands of a child; but if consolidated into a rock, it mocks the united efforts of mankind, and can only fall in a general wreck of nature.

Republicus.

# Document 6

# Amendment 12

*Manner of Choosing a President and Vice-President*
*This Amendment altered Article 2 Section 1 Part 2*
*Passed by Congress December 9, 1803. Ratified July 27, 1804.*

1. The Electors shall meet in their respective States and vote by ballot for President and Vice-President, one of whom, at least, shall not be an inhabitant of the same State with themselves; they shall name in their ballots the person voted for as President, and in distinct ballots the person voted for as Vice-President, and of the number of votes for each, which lists they shall sign and certify, and transmit sealed to the seat of the Government of the United States, directed to the President of the Senate; the President of the Senate shall, in the presence of the Senate and House of Representatives, open all the certificates and the votes shall then be counted; - The person having the greatest number of votes for President, shall be the President, if such number be a majority of the whole number of Electors appointed; and if no person have such majority, then from the persons having the highest numbers not exceeding three on the list of those voted for as President, the House of Representatives shall choose immediately, by ballot, the President. But in choosing the President, the votes shall be taken by States, the representation from each State having one vote; a quorum for this purpose shall consist of a member or members from two-thirds of the States, and a majority of all the States shall be necessary to a choice. *And if the House of Representatives shall not choose a President whenever the right of choice shall devolve upon them, before the fourth day of March next following, then the Vice-President shall act as President, as in case of the death or other constitutional disability of the President.* (The words in italics were superseded by Amendment XX)

3. The person having the greatest number of votes as Vice-President, shall be the Vice-President, if such numbers be a majority of the whole number of electors appointed, and if no person have a majority, then from the two highest numbers on the list, the Senate shall choose the Vice-President; a quorum for the purpose shall consist of two-thirds of the whole number of Senators, and a majority of the whole number shall be necessary to a choice. But no person constitutionally ineligible to the office of President shall be eligible to that of Vice-President of the United States.

# Documents 7

# Timothy Pickering, Speech in Favor of the Twelfth Amendement

*Timothy Pickering, [Speech in favor of the twelfth amendment], circa October 17, 1803. (The Gilder Lehrman Institute of American History, GLC05321.02)*

Mr Speaker -,

The People, by their Electors shall elect the President, this is undoubtedly the meaning and the true constriction given the Constitution,- then to carry this fully into effect is doubtless pursuing the wishes of the framers of that Instrument: - and I contend that the Amendment under consideration is calculated to accomplish this object and without this amendment, a person not having the confidence of the Nation may be elected - can it be said with this contingent, that the Constitution will inspire so full confidence as if [inserted: the] difficulty was removed. -Confidence in a Republican government is important, confidence cannot be placed in such a government if the majority cannot govern. - , But, Sir, we are told that certain great States are determined to use up all authority and bear down the constitution; that the very place where we are now [at] is to become Virginia property, and therefore we must not tutch that sacred instrument the constitution. - and, Sir if this be so: Suppose at the time of the late Presidental [sic] election, no President had been elected untill after the fourth of March - who would answer for the consequences? would not the great States then have refused (in agreeing to a new Constitution which must then have been formed) to give the small States an equal vote with the larger in the Senate, - and this precious article in the present Constitution cannot ever be altered - privelages enjoyid under the present constitution are much greater than could be expected were a new Constitution now to be formed, - to prevent the Constitution from running out by the present amendment is of more importance to the Small States, than can possibly ever be gained to them by, electing a President under the Constitution as it now is. –

[2] I believe, Sir we outfit not to calculate to turn, or have a wish for the election of a President, in any other way than by the Electors, for without this popular privelage the constitution would not have been adopted - again four small States which send but Eight members to the House of representatives have a right to Sixteen votes for President while a great State, having a right to send say from 18 to 25 Members can add but two to her number in the choice of a President is [inserted: not] this advantage great enough for small States in that particular, under such an institution. -, On the subject of innovation, great clamour is made. I am not infavor of innovation or amendments except for important and mighty considerations; - but were not amendments expected: most certainly they were expected and I will venture & say that without this provision, the constitution would never have been adopted. - And will any Gent.n Say that amendments have as yet injured the constitution: it is a well known fact that the amendments already incorporated into the constitution have greatly increased its friends. - One Gentn afraid this amendment will also increase its friends, and stability and in that way prevent and destroy a favorite object with [Lernes], namly , a division of the Union between the northern and southern States}- I will not accuse any gentn. In this house with such base motion but Sir I believe there are men base enough in New England to wish for such a measure., Under an impression that the proposed amendment if adopted will give Stability and duration to the Constitution I shall give it my hearty support - ,

[docket], Legislature 1804

# Document 8

# James Madison to George Hay

*from* The Writings of James Madison. *Edited by Gaillard Hunt. 9 vols.*
*New York: G. P. Putnam's Sons, 1900-1910.*

*23 Aug. 1823*

I have received your letter of the 11th, with the Newspapers containing your remarks on the present mode of electing a President, and your proposed remedy for its defects. I am glad to find you have not abandoned your attention to great Constitutional topics. The difficulty of finding an unexceptionable process for appointing the Executive Organ of a Government such as that of the U.S. was deeply felt by the Convention; and as the final arrangement of it took place in the latter stage of the Session, it was not exempt from a degree of the hurrying influence produced by fatigue and impatience in all such Bodies, tho' the degree was much less than usually prevails in them.

The part of the arrangement which casts the eventual appointment on the House of Reps. voting by States, was, as you presume, an accommodation to the anxiety of the smaller States for their sovereign equality, and to the jealousy of the larger towards the cumulative functions of the Senate. The agency of the H. of Reps. was thought safer also than that of the Senate, on account of the greater number of its members. It might indeed happen that the event would turn on one or two States having one or two Reps. only; but even in that case, the representations of most of the States being numerous, the House would present greater obstacles to corruption than the Senate with its paucity of Members. It may be observed also, that altho' for a certain period the evil of State votes given by one or two individuals would be extended by the introduction of new States, it would be rapidly diminished by growing populations within extensive territories. At the present period, the evil is at its maximum. Another Census will leave none of the States existing or in Embryo, in the numerical rank of R.I. & Del, nor is it impossible, that the progressive assimilation of local Institutions, laws & manners, may[Volume 3, Page 557] overcome the prejudices of those particular States against an incorporation with their neighbours.

But with all possible abatements the present rule of voting for President by the H. of Reps. is so great a departure from the Republican principle of numerical equality, and even from the federal rule which qualifies the numerical by a State equality, and is so pregnant also with a mischievous tendency in practice, that an amendment of the Constitution on this point is justly called for by all its considerate & best friends.

I agree entirely with you in thinking that the election of Presidential Electors by districts, is an amendment very proper to be brought forward at the same time with that relating to the eventual choice of President by the H. of Reps. The district mode was mostly, if not exclusively in view when the Constitution was framed and adopted; & was exchanged for the general ticket & the legislative election, as the only expedient for baffling the policy of the particular States which had set the example. A constitutional establishment of that mode will doubtless aid in reconciling the smaller States to the other change which they will regard as a concession on their part. And it may not be without a value in another important respect. The States when voting for President by general tickets or by their Legislatures, are a string of beads; when they make their elections by districts, some of these differing in sentiment from others, and sympathizing with that of districts in other States, they are so knit together as to break the force of those geographical and other noxious parties which might render the repulsive too strong for the cohesive tendencies within the Political System.

It may be worthy of consideration whether in requiring elections by districts, a discretion might not be conveniently left with the States to allot two members to a single district. It would manifestly be an important proviso, that no new arrangement of districts should be made within a certain period previous to an ensuing election of President.

Of the different remedies you propose for the failure of a majority of Electoral votes for any one Candidate, I like best that which refers the final choice, to a joint vote of the two Houses of Congress, restricted to the two highest names on the Electoral lists. It might be a question, whether the three instead of the two highest names might not be put within the choice of Congress, inasmuch as it not unfrequently happens, that the Candidate third on the list of votes would in a question with either of the two first outvote him, and, consequently be the real preference of the voters. But this advantage of opening a wider door & a better chance to merit, may be outweighed by an increased difficulty in obtaining a prompt & quiet decision by Congress with three candidates before them, supported by three parties, no one of them making a majority of the whole.

The mode which you seem to approve, of making a plurality of Electoral votes a definitive appointment would have the merit of avoiding the Legislative agency in appointing the Executive; but might it not, by multiplying hopes and chances, stimulate intrigue & exertion, as well as incur too great a risk of success to a very inferior candidate? Next to the propriety of having a President the real choice of a majority of his Constituents, it is desirable that he should inspire respect & acquiescence by qualifications not suffering too much by comparison.

I cannot but think also that there is a strong objection to undistinguishing votes for President & Vice President; the highest number appointing the former the next the latter. To say nothing of the different services (except in a rare contingency) which are to be performed by them, occasional transpositions would take place, violating equally the mutual consciousness of the individuals, & the public estimate of their comparative fitness.

Having thus made the remarks to which your communication led, with a frankness which I am sure you will not disapprove, whatever errors you may find in them, I will sketch for your consideration a substitute which has occurred to myself for the faulty part of the Constitution in question

"The Electors to be chosen in districts, not more than two in any one district, and the arrangement of the districts not to be alterable within the period of ------ previous to the election of President. Each Elector to give two votes, one naming his first choice, the other his next choice. If there be a majority of all the votes on the first list for the same person, he of course to be President; if not, and there be a majority, (which may well happen) on the other list for the same person, he then to be the final choice; if there be no such majority on either list, then a choice to be made by joint ballot of the two Houses of Congress, from the two names having the greatest number of votes on the two lists taken together." Such a process would avoid the inconvenience of a second resort to the Electors; and furnish a double chance of avoiding an eventual resort to Congress. The same process might be observed in electing the Vice President.

Your letter found me under some engagements which have retarded a compliance with its request, and may have also rendered my view of the subject presented in it more superficial than I have been aware. This consideration alone would justify my wish not to be brought into the public discussion. But there is another in the propensity of the Moment, to view everything, however abstract from the Presidential election in prospect, thro' a medium connecting it with that question; a propensity the less to be excused as no previous change of the Constitution can be contemplated, and the more to be regretted, as opinions and commitments formed under its influence, may become settled obstacles at a practicable season.

# Document 9

# James Madison to John Hillhouse

*from* The Writings of James Madison. *Edited by Gaillard Hunt. 9 vols. New York: G. P. Putnam's Sons, 1900-1910.*

*Montpr*
*May 1830.*

Dear Sir

I have received your letter of the 10th inst: with the pamphlet containing the proposed amendments of the Constitution of the U. States, on which you request my opinion & remarks.

Whatever pleasure might be felt in a fuller compliance with your request, I must avail myself of the pleas of the age I have reached, and of the controul of other engagements, for not venturing on more than the few observations suggested by a perusal of what you have submitted to the public.

I readily acknowledge the ingenuity which devised the plan you recommend, and the strength of reasoning [367] with which you support it. I cannot however but regard it as liable to the following remarks:

1. The first that occurs is, that the large States would not exchange the proportional agency they now have in the appointment of the Chief Magistrate, for a mode placing the largest & smallest States on a perfect equality in that cardinal transaction. N. York has in it, even now more than 13 times the weight of several of the States, and other States according to their magnitudes wd decide on the change with correspondent calculations & feelings.

The difficulty of reconciling the larger States to the equality in the Senate is known to have been the most threatning that was encountered in framing the Constitution. It is known also that the powers committed to that body, comprehending, as they do, Legislative, Ex. & Judicial functions, was among the most serious objections, with many, to the adoption of the Constitution.

2. As the President elect would generally be without any previous evidence of national confidence, and have been in responsible relations only to a particular State, there might be danger of State partialities, and a certainty of injurious suspicions of them.

3. Considering the ordinary composition of the Senate, and the number (in a little time nearly 50) out of which a single one was to be taken by pure chance; it must often happen, that the winner of the prize would want some of the qualities necessary to command the respect of the nation, and possibly be [368] marked with some of an opposite tendency. On a review of the composition of that Body thro' the successive periods of its existence, (antecedent to the present which may be an exception) how often will names present themselves, which would be seen with mortified feelings at the head of the nation. It might happen, it is true, that, in the choice of Senators, an eventual elevation to that important trust might produce more circumspection in the State Legislatures. But so remote a contingency could not be expected to have any great influence; besides that there might be States not furnishing at the time, characters which would satisfy the pride and inspire the confidence of the States & of the People.

4. A President not appointed by the nation and without the weight derived from its selection & confidence, could not afford the advantage expected from the qualified negative on the act of the Legislative branch of the Govt. He might either shrink from the delicacy of such an interposition, or it might be overruled with too little hesitation by the body checked in its career.

5. In the vicissitudes of party, adverse views & feelings will exist between the Senate & President. Under the amendments proposed, a spirit of opposition in the former to the latter would probably be more frequent than heretofore. In such a state of things, how apt might the Senate be to embarrass the President, by refusing to concur in the removal of an obnoxious officer; how prone would be

a refractory [369] officer, having powerful friends in the Senate, to take shelter under that authority, & bid defiance to the President; and, with such discord and anarchy in the Ex. Department, how impaired would be the security for a due execution of the Laws!

6. On the supposition that the above objection would be overbalanced by the advantage of reducing the power and the patronage now attached to the Presidential office; it has generally been admitted, that the Heads of Depts at least who are at once the associates & the organs of the Chief Magistrate, ought to be well disposed towards him, and not independent of him. What would be the situation of the President, and what might be the effect on the Executive business, if those immediately around him, and in daily consultation with him, could, however adverse to him in their feelings & their views, be fastened upon him, by a Senate disposed to take side with them? The harmony so expedient between the P. & Heads of Departments, and among the latter themselves, has been too liable to interruption under an organization apparently so well providing against it.

I am aware that some of these objections might be mitigated, if not removed; but not I suspect in a degree to render the proposed modification of the Executive Department an eligible substitute for the one existing. At the same time, I am duly sensible of the evils incident to the existing one, and that a solid improvement of it is a desideratum that ought to be welcomed by all enlightened patriots.

In the mean time, I cannot feel all the alarm you express at the prospect for the future as reflected from the mirror of the past. It will be a rare case that the Presidential contest will not issue in a choice that will not discredit the station, and not be acquiesced in by the unsuccessful party, foreseeing, as it must do, the appeal to be again made at no very distant day to the will of the nation. As long as the country shall be exempt from a military force powerful in itself and combined with a powerful faction, liberty & peace will find safeguards in the elective resource and the spirit of the people. The dangers which threaten our political system least remote are perhaps of other sorts and from other sources.

I will only add to these remarks, what is indeed sufficiently evident, that they are too hasty & too crude for any other than a private, and that an indulgent eye.

Mrs. M. is highly gratified by your kind expressions towards her, & begs you to be assured that she still feels for you that affectionate friendship with which you impressed her many years ago. Permit me to join her in best wishes for your health & every other happiness.

James Madison
May 1830 Montpellier
M. L. Hurlbert

# Contributors

**Eric Burin** is Professor of History at the University of North Dakota, and author of *Slavery and the Peculiar Solution: A History of the American Colonization Society* (2005).

**Brad Austin** is Professor of history at Salem State University, where he also serves as his department's secondary education co-ordinator. He is the author of *Democratic Sports: Men's and Women's College Sports During the Great Depression* (Arkansas) and the co-editor of *Understanding and Teaching the Vietnam War* (Wisconsin). He is a series editor for the University of Wisconsin Press's Harvey Goldberg Series for Understanding and Teaching History.

**William Caraher** is an Associate Professor in History at the University of North Dakota. His is the co-author of *The Bakken: An Archaeology of an Industrial Landscape* (2017) with Bret Weber and co-author of *Pyla-Koutsopetria I:Archaeological Survey of An Ancient Coastal Town* (2014) with R. Scott Moore and David K. Pettegrew.

**Allen C. Guelzo** is the Henry R. Luce Professor of the Civil War Era at Gettysburg College, and the author of several books on Abraham Lincoln and the American Civil War.

**James H. Hulme** is an attorney in private practice in Washington, D.C.

**Mark Stephen Jendrysik** is a Professor in the Department of Political Science and Public Administration at the University of North Dakota. His research focuses on contemporary American political culture and on the intersections of utopian thought and politics. He is the author of *Modern Jeremiahs: Contemporary Visions of American Decline* (Rowman and Littlefield, 2008).

**Donald F. Johnson** is an assistant professor at North Dakota State University. His research focuses on popular politics during the era of the American Revolution.

**Benjamin J. Kassow** is an assistant professor in the Department of Political Science and Public Administration. His research focuses on judicial institutions within the United States, with a particular focus on U.S. Courts of Appeals, as well as state courts of last resort. His teaching interests lie in teaching courses on American government, as well as constitutional law and courses related to the United States judiciary.

**Andrew Meyer** is Associate Professor of History at Brooklyn College, CUNY. His field is early Chinese intellectual history, and he is the author of *The Dao of the Military: Liu An's Art of War*.

**Cynthia Culver Prescott** is an associate professor of History at the University of North Dakota. Her research focuses on gender, material culture and memory in the American West.

**Timothy Prescott** is an Associate Professor of Mathematics at the University of North Dakota. His research focuses on probability, random walks, and evolving sets.

**Patrick Rael** is Professor of History at Bowdoin College in Brunswick, Maine. His most recent book is *Eighty-Eight Years: The Long Death of Slavery in the United States, 1777-1865* (Athens, GA: University of Georgia Press, 2015).

**Andrew Shankman** is Associate Professor of History at Rutgers University-Camden and has authored and edited several books and essays treating the Early American Republic. His most recent book is *Original Intents: Hamilton, Jefferson, Madison, and the American Founding*, published by Oxford University Press in 2017.

**Manisha Sinha** is the Draper Chair in American History at the University of Connecticut. Her book, *The Slave's Cause: A History of Abolition*, was long listed for the National Book Award for Nonfiction.

**Mark Trahant** is the Charles R. Johnson Endowed Professor of Journalism at the University of North Dakota. He blogs at trahantreports.com

**Jack Russell Weinstein** is Chester Fritz Distinguished Professor of Philosophy and Director if the Institute for Philosophy in Public Life at the University of North Dakota. He is the host of the long-running philosophy radio show and podcast *Why? Philosophical Discussions About Everyday Life*; his most recent book *Adam Smith's Pluralism: Rationality, Education and the Moral Sentiments*, was published by Yale University Press.

Made in the USA
Coppell, TX
02 July 2020

30036339R00085